REINVENTING TRAINING
AND DEVELOPMENT

REINVENTING TRAINING
AND DEVELOPMENT

Ronald R. Sims

Q

QUORUM BOOKS
Westport, Connecticut · London

Library of Congress Cataloging-in-Publication Data

Sims, Ronald R.
    Reinventing training and development / Ronald R. Sims.
        p.   cm.
    Includes bibliographical references and index.
    ISBN 1–56720–180–6 (alk. paper)
    1. Employees, Training of.   2. Occupational training.
    3. Training.   I. Title.
    HF5549.5.T7S5574   1998
    658.3'12404—dc21   98–20132

British Library Cataloguing in Publication Data is available.

Library of Congress Catalog Card Number: 98–20132
ISBN: 1–56720–180–6

First published in 1998

Quorum Books, 88 Post Road West, Westport, CT 06881
An imprint of Greenwood Publishing Group, Inc.

Printed in the United States of America

∞™

The paper used in this book complies with the
Permanent Paper Standard issued by the National
Information Standards Organization (Z39.48–1984).

10   9   8   7   6   5   4   3   2   1

To Serbrenia, Ronald, Jr., Marchet, Vellice,
Nandi, Dangaia, and Sieya

Contents

Illustrations

Preface

Over the years I have been fortunate to experience training and development in several ways. First and most importantly, as a training professional and consultant for many years, I struggled directly with the growth, decline, and reemergence of training as I worked with a variety of organizations to help them improve their training initiatives and staff. Second, as an educator in a school of business, I viewed training and development from a different perspective as a disseminator of knowledge and facilitator of learning about the topic. Third, as an experienced author and researcher, I explored, examined, and reported on this topic for a number of years. Fourth, as an officer in the military, I viewed training and development from a completely different perspective. Finally, as a participant in many training and development efforts, I have been able to experience and appreciate being a benefactor of some very excellent trainers and programs.

From these varied perspectives, several impressions begin to emerge about the training profession, all underscoring the need for continued change or reinvention of the training function. Collectively, these perspectives provided a unique vantage point from which to write this book. The final product should be a valuable contribution to help training professionals and their organizations to continue the process of improving the training contribution in order to achieve an organization's strategic agenda.

A major point of this book is that training and development will continue to become more and more important to organizational success. In the future, it will not be enough for training professionals to stay on top of the latest improvements in training and development, given the rapid pace of change in organizations. In the era of increased accountability, it becomes even more important for training functions to be more proactive in demonstrating their value to the organization, and to be more responsive to customer needs. More than ever, training functions must pay as much attention to how they are changing as they do to the changes in their host organizations and the larger world.

The primary audience for this book is practicing trainers, human resource professionals, and organizational leaders. The book provides tested and proven ideas important to demonstrating the value of training. From a practical viewpoint, it is based on actual experiences, a strong research base, and accepted practices presented in a systematic format.

A second target audience is students of training and development and human resources who are preparing for careers in this important field. This book will help them develop a solid foundation to the study of training and development practices that are key to training and organization success.

A third target audience is middle and top level leaders who want to know more about how training and development can contribute to organizational success. It offers leaders a firsthand look at what they should expect of their training function and how they can encourage the training staff to become regular contributors to the organization.

This book focuses on reinventing training by discussing the importance of taking a strategic approach to accomplish its mission. More specifically, Chapter 1 lays the foundation for the ideas presented in the remainder of the book, as it highlights the importance of reinventing training by discussing a number of attributes of reinvented training. Chapter 2 presents a strategic approach to training and the needs analysis phase of training. Chapter 3 focuses on a model for designing training initiatives. Chapter 4 emphasizes the importance of training methods (or technologies) to the successful design and implementation of training and development initiatives. The changing role of management (leadership) development is the focus of Chapter 5. Chapter 6 describes the role of debriefing in enhancing transfer of learning back to the work situation. Chapters 7 and 8 present information on issues important to the design and implementation of training evaluation. Chapter 9 discusses the future of training and development.

Acknowledgments

While a single name is often given as the author of a publication like this, it is hardly a solitary effort. Many colleagues who are training professionals have shared their ideas, which have been refined and developed, and ultimately presented here. To all of them, I owe much appreciation for their contribution.

My continued appreciation and thanks are extended to Herrington Bryce, the Life Insurance of Virginia Professor at the School of Business Administration, College of William and Mary, who, as my dear friend and mentor, constantly encourages me to grow and develop. The College of William and Mary and the School of Business Administration deserve considerable recognition for their cooperation and wholehearted support of this undertaking by providing opportunities for the author to conduct the research required to complete this book.

Many thanks to Terry Trojak, Phyllis Viands, and Sherry Thomas, support staff of the School of Business Administration who continue to work with me in the production process. Finally, I owe much appreciation to my wife Serbrenia and our daughters, Nandi, Dangaia, and Sieya, who provide encouragement, support, and assistance on all of my efforts, including this book. They always make many sacrifices for me to pursue my work.

CHAPTER 1

Training and Development Today and Tomorrow

"We are entering a world where the old rules no longer apply." The opening quote in the bestseller *Rising Sun* by Michael Crichton (1992) sums up how rapidly the future is changing and becoming unpredictable. Given the commitment to the continuous changes taking place in all types of organizations, like their host human resource (HR) functions, change will be the only certainty for training functions and those responsible for training and development initiatives in their organizations. Training functions will have to run differently as organizations expect more evidence that they are contributing to organizational success. In response to calls for changes in the way training has traditionally been done, many have responded by calling for redefining the mission of training, renaming training (i.e., witness the recent movement to referring to training and development professionals as "performance consultants"—Robinson & Robinson 1995), and even firing or getting rid of in-house training altogether because it is not cost-effective (see Furnham 1997 for a more detailed discussion of this last point). In short, the pressure is on for trainers and training functions to reinvent, reengineer, revitalize, remake, and improve what they do (Shandler 1996).

The primary objective of this chapter is to provide a foundation for the ideas presented in this book and to answer the following question: What are some of the attributes of reinvented training? In answering this question, this chapter will provide a detailed discussion of a number of attributes important to making changes in training in today's and tomorrow's organizations. The chapter will first briefly discuss some issues requiring the training function to shed its traditional role.

ISSUES IMPACTING THE TRAINING FUNCTION AND PROFESSION

Organizations are still focusing on reinvention and reengineering as they continue to place greater emphasis upon improving customer service. This increased attention to customer service is expected despite downsizing and delaying efforts in the organization.

The strength of these trends is likely to continue even if the names change from time to time, for the changes emerge from a growing realization that traditional ways of doing business and being organized prevents an organization from moving fast enough, with high enough quality, or at low enough cost to meet the growing demands and competitive pressures placed on it.

The next decade will continue to witness major changes in organizations. Organizations will continue to get flatter, and power will be more dispersed among employees who are knowledge workers and have the technology to make decisions previously reserved for management. As Harlan Cleveland (1985) noted, if information is power, then dispersed information is dispersed power, and that dispersement is what knowledge and technology does. There will also continue to be an increased emphasis upon the use of cross-functional and multiskilled teams, which are essential in taking advantage of advanced technologies, and these developments should free the smaller number of managers to focus on higher level strategic issues.

The boundaries that have traditionally defined organizations will continue to blur as a result of new organizational forms and leadership methods and demands. The lines between functions and even between organizations will continue to become less rigid in the drive to be more customer focused, to decrease response and work process cycle times, and improve competitive advantage. The distinction between types of organizations (large versus small, regional versus national versus global) will also begin to blur more as customers show less interest in where their products and services come from as long as they receive them when and at the standards of quality they deem acceptable.

We are also likely to see a continued increase in the use of telecommuters, part-time workers, and cooperative education and apprenticeship students, so that the meaning of the word "employee" will become less clear. Also, the increasing use of outsourcing and the involvement of both customers and vendors in coproducing products and services are yet other trends that will force training professionals to ask basic questions about who the customer is, what they need, and what development means in an ever changing organization and workforce.

All these changes will thrust some people out of leadership roles and far more people into them (as all employees are expected to think and act like leaders) whether they carry the title of leader or not. They will require leadership behavior that continues to be much more widely dispersed in today's and tomorrow's organizations. Training and development professionals will be called upon to be consultants, policysetters, value purveyors, leaders, and facilitators of this and other organizational changes.

THE TRAINING PROFESSION AND FUNCTION

The training, or human resource development (HRD), profession is much more advanced and sophisticated than it was twenty-five years ago, when many of us had our initial experiences as practitioners. It is the contention of this book that this is a great era for those in the profession because of our increased capabilities and the expanding opportunities we have to serve our organizations.

Some of us have perceived the dramatic changes in our work environment as threats to the profession. We've faced many new developments: competition from other providers of training and development services; new developments in training technology that are revolutionizing the training processes; management philosophies that emphasize increased accountability and a broader role for the training function; and a conscious movement away from training for training's sake to more real-time and cost-effective training.

While such developments may have seemed ominous, they have proven to be catalysts for positive change. We've been challenged to reassess our roles in today's organizations and to use our capability and potential to help the organization grow, develop, and transform itself. When the history of this chapter of training and development is written, I think it will attribute much of this development to the fact that we have embraced quality, continuous improvement, and customer service concepts that have become widely popular in business during this time.

Is there an internal training function today that is not regularly assessing itself by asking these fundamental questions?

- Are we focused and aligned with our customers?
- Is our service delivery cost-effective and timely?
- Do we anticipate our customer's needs?
- Do we provide consistent delivery of value-added benefits?

Perhaps we do understand our ability to reinvent ourselves. Many training functions have begun to establish the foundation for the future by redefining training practices in these terms and are well positioned to move on, but we must be prepared to anticipate the need for further change.

We can best anticipate and respond to the need for further change in training by remembering that training historically has been looked at as a case-by-case, individual perspective, much like the way a doctor looks at a patient. You do a diagnosis of an individual, find a weakness, and then apply the training solution so that individual is stronger or better than he or she was before. What training must be in today's and tomorrow's organizations is a process that is more holistic, and consistent with an organization's strategy, so that the strategy is executed better than it would be without the training. One strategy is individual, which will have no impact on an organization, and the other is corporate, which will have a mammoth impact.

The important thing for training personnel to conceptually understand is that training must have an impact on the organization rather than on the individual. The point is to make the organization more whole than it was before, and training should be a major part of what causes that to happen. However, that will never happen if training personnel are doing training by picking up people and putting bandaids on cuts. It will only do it if there is a vision and a strategy, and training is part of a process of executing that vision and strategy for everyone.

We must also be attentive to the fact that just applying technology to the training systems we have today is not going to solve the kinds of problems and challenges affecting training functions and their organizations, especially if all we do is take a system that doesn't produce the results we want and make it more difficult, which will only make things worse than some believe they already are.

As training professionals we must remember that training isn't an event. Training is not something out of a box. Training is a continuous process linked to all the ways that people are developed: by their job challenges; by their interactions with the people who are in coaching roles with them; by their peers; and by something we call training.

And if it is out of a box, now technology can help us. So training becomes more continuous. It becomes more online. It can be individualized, but in a strategic context, it can help the organization achieve its goals. Technology has to be seen as a tool inside a much broader context of helping the organization develop its employees.

We must also be committed to getting valid, reliable, and credible measures of customer satisfaction and employee satisfaction. Training and development personnel must get these measures into the organization to the right people in a timely way. The problem is that, unlike a lot of financial reporting that is done, satisfaction measures are often one-time events—a single survey done once every twelve to eighteen months. They are not systemic, ongoing, continual processes that are plugged in at different levels in the organization.

Finally, at some point we need to spend less time trying to come up with a term (or terms) that is all inclusive of what we do in training. The real challenge appears to be spending more time making sure we can clearly communicate what we actually do that contributes to achievement of the organization's strategic agenda. The emergence of what is now known as human resource development (HRD) appears to be a move in the right direction, since it, as it is currently practiced, is an extension of the traditional activities of the training function. While there have been a number of recent efforts to rename trainers and training functions to reflect increased or changing responsibilities, as the label HRD does, for purposes of this book we will still use the traditional terms of trainers and the training function. This is not to say that concepts like performance consulting (consultants), HRD professionals, and other labels may not be more appropriate, but for our purposes, trainers or training professionals and training functions will be used to refer to such terms as HRD, or training and development.

THE ENVIRONMENT FOR EXCELLENCE

It has been said that doing an excellent job is much more satisfying than doing a mediocre job. As training professionals, we need to do everything in our power to provide environments that aren't satisfied with mediocrity—that strive for excellence, not only in training, but throughout the organization. And this mandate isn't just the responsibility of training; it's for everyone who participates in any training, learning, or development initiatives.

Achieving organizational excellence is linked to defining values. When training is based on a set of shared values that meshes with the mission of the organization, a culture that is energized and continually driven towards excellence can prevail. Much of what we do as training professionals supports and validates what the organization has determined to be important by its values. Training in the context of an organization's values becomes much more relevant to all involved.

As a profession, we must continue to strive for excellence and work toward reinvention of our profession and the training function. For our purposes, the use of the word reinvention implies a number of things. First, the reinvention process is a means to an end in transforming the way an organization (and in our case trainers and the training function) conducts its key business activities. Second, reinvention can imply either starting over from scratch with the fundamental ways things are done, or simply changing the way things are done without having to start over. Trainers and training functions that start over from scratch forget all about how work was performed in the past, and start all over with a clean sheet of paper, thinking about how things can be done best right now. When trainers use the latter form of reinvention they also think about how things can be done better through innovation. In either case, reinvention is concerned with both best practices and benchmarking.

The third main focus of reinvention is the customer. Everything that is done starts with the idea of adding value for the customer: improving service, raising quality, and lowering costs. Finally, reinvention suggests a planned process of change in response to changes in the host environment (i.e., the organization and HR function). Achieving such change will in many instances require changes in the trainers and training functions in terms of identity, strategy, structure, and culture, and the institutionalization of new and better ways of accomplishing their charge.

ATTRIBUTES OF REINVENTED TRAINING

This section provides a discussion of the attributes and necessary characteristics of reinvented training. The four attributes (strategic orientation, customer orientation, performance improvement orientation, and accountability orientation) are discussed in the following sections, as well as a description of the necessary characteristics of a training program that has been reinvented, such as quality design, timeliness, cost-effectiveness, flexibility, and a means for evaluation.

Strategic Orientation

Reinvented training is a catalyst for and a catalyst of improvement in an organization and achievement of the organization's strategic agenda. Thus, reinvented training must be inextricably woven into the clarity of the organization's mission, strategic agenda, its human resources systems, and its culture. Like its host organization, HR function means that the training function scans the internal environment to stay abreast of changes in strategies and the direction of the organization, the needs and characteristics of the workforce, and the needs of senior executives and other managers as they seek to make their organizations and its human resources more productive, flexible, adaptable, and focused.

Combining the internal, organizational characteristics with the external conditions, training professionals must help their organizations develop employees who are adaptable, committed, motivated, and highly energetic, and are good performers in diverse groups. They also need to be good team players, as well as be multiskilled or reskilled knowledge workers. In short, reinvented training is linked to the HRD mission, practices, and priorities, and to the organization's strategy. It is more macro than micro, supports the organization's strategic directions, and is thus strategic in nature itself.

In helping the organization achieve its goals, reinvented training takes a strategic approach and looks at the training mission and concomitant processes in a radically different light. This strategic approach to training takes place within an overall framework for workforce development that directly contributes to the organization's achievement of its mission while also revolutionizing its processes. Reinvented training eliminates misaligned goals and objectives between training functions and their host organizations. Reinvented training must identify the training that is critical, if organizations are to accomplish their mission, by identifying (1) what training is currently done that is no longer needed, (2) what training can be eliminated altogether, (3) how the remaining training can be better linked to support and reinforce the organization's strategic agenda, (4) what new training should be offered, and (5) what nontraining initiatives should be undertaken. In the end, reinvented training must be "rebuilt" based on the basics— the actual training required to accomplish the fundamental organizational purpose, versus the processes that have evolved over time.

Reinvented training provides a clear understanding of the characteristics of and requirements for a strategic approach to training that will have an impact on the parent organization. Such a perspective forms connections between training missions and practices, HR missions and practices, and the organization's missions and practices. The premise behind strategic training is that training decisions that fit the organization's current and future conditions positively impact performance.

Customer Orientation

Reinvented training means encouraging and responding to customer inputs in designing and implementing value-added training. Reinvented training is always looking for ways to involve customers by asking them what they want, when they want it, and how training can better meet their needs. Existing processes for partnering with customers are viewed in a radically different light, and efforts are continually in motion to get closer to the customer. Like today's proactive organizations, reinvented training functions step back and ask the question, How can we get closer to the customer and bring them further into the work, learning, training, and development design processes?

In answering this question, reinvented training begins by partnering with customers to ensure that *all* training is indeed seen by the customer as adding value. Adding value requires that the customers be seen as experts and their needs determine the what, when, how, and where of training.

Reinvented training is driven by a proactive goal of exceeding customer expectations. It requires encouraging the participation of customer groups in identifying necessary employee knowledge, skills, abilities, and other characteristics (KSAOCs) and competencies and corresponding training needs, and in designing, implementing, and evaluating training strategies. By tapping into the considerable expertise of customers, the training function further conforms to the organization's strategy. At every level of activity, the training function puts the customer first, views customers as experts, regularly communicates with customers to understand their needs, and uses customer input to make training more effective.

Performance Improvement Orientation

Reinvented training is concerned with the way in which training supports employees within the organization to perform at their highest levels so that the entire organization can perform at its highest level. Reinvented training must do two things to fulfill this role: (1) support the work done right now in the organization by providing training at the place it is needed, at the time it is needed, and in the amount and strength it is needed; and (2) support the work to be done in the future by creating a learning infrastructure that will help employees and the organization learn and grow and change in line with environmental demands.

The dual mission—support the organization now, and help the organization prepare for the future—means that training functions must identify critical workforce KSAOCs and competencies and must design training initiatives that help employees develop those KSAOCs and competencies. For example, today's and tomorrow's organizations need employees that are multiskilled/reskilled knowledge workers who can effectively work in teams. Thus, meeting these new standards requires that training divisions recognize the need for a workforce that is more than just technically trained. It requires training people who are capable of analyzing and solving job-related problems, and of being able to "switch gears" and shift from job to job. Reinvented training thus is moved to center stage as a means of improving organization performance.

In response to calls for radical change in organizations, some organizations are streamlining procedures so that fewer employees are needed to get the work done. Such broad-based approaches provide a framework for reinvented training aimed at improving employee and organization performance. Reinvented training prepares employees to better work in teams, identify and make recommendations for eliminating low-value work, correct inefficient work processes, and improve product and service quality through cost efficiencies. Reinvented training also teaches employees to examine and evaluate tasks and processes, rather than accepting jobs as they are currently configured. Reinvented training is "best practices" and "benchmarking" oriented in its efforts to respond to customers' needs for quality, variety, customization, convenience, and timeliness.

Accountability Orientation

In today's environment, reinvented training functions must be able to prove that they have quality designs (including a systematic rather than a piecemeal approach, and the effective use of the best available technology and alternative training methods), timeliness, cost-effectiveness, flexibility (including using the most effective providers), and means for evaluation.

Reinvented training is committed to increasing its capacity and flexibility for delivering just-in-time and cost-effective training that can be easily evaluated by training customers and training personnel. This means, for example, that training moves beyond its focus on the creation of discrete training courses to develop much more flexibility and variety in its training programs, to identify more cost-effective and alternative means to bring training and learning opportunities into the organization (thus closer to the employee), and, at the same time, to find ways to hold itself accountable (through ongoing evaluation of its training efforts) for the training objectives it seeks to achieve.

Like their host HR functions, many training functions have traditionally been largely insulated from competition and accountability and in many instances have enjoyed a monopoly by being the "only game in town" for their customers. In contrast, reinvented training is built upon the view that (1) the training function no longer has a monopoly to provide training for organization employees, and (2) competition is the name of the game, as customers will go to those who are best able to meet their training needs. So, just as increasing competition and loss of customers fostered the climate of reinvention for many organizations, the recent emergence of these factors on the training scene has created a customer accountability environment for the training function.

Quality Design

Training functions must recognize the need to rethink the way they have provided training to their customers. This is most evident with increased efforts to explore ways of bringing training closer to the employee, to use available technology, and to find alternative ways of delivering training.

Improvement of training efforts should be based on the belief that training should use a systems approach any time new training is designed. This type of approach brings the training closer to the customer, better addresses training needs, and improves both the cost-effectiveness and efficiency of training.

Reinvented training designs and delivers training and other learning efforts (e.g., leadership development) that are based on tried and tested models of learning, such as Kolb's experiential learning model discussed in Chapter 3. The use of such models increase the likelihood of learning occurring, and the transfer of learning back to the work situation, as increased attention is focused on debriefing the learning experiences of participants and the development of action plans to increase back-at-work application of training learning.

Where appropriate, reinvented training increasingly uses training hardware technology to deliver training, through systems like distance learning. Distance learning systems might include multimedia elements, video teletraining, and the capacity to link them in various configurations in combination with on-site or commuting distance classroom facilities. Such a system can also link them with correspondence courses, academia, and other parts of particular industries.

Reinvented training recognizes that new training technology could dramatically improve their training processes. Examples are increased use of distance learning, CD-ROM, Inter- and Intranet, and simulations in delivering training. The increased emphasis on alternative ways of delivering training is a result of realizing the need to move away from an instructor–classroom-dependent design of training to more just-in-time training. The above initiatives should lead to better measurement of the impact of training, training responsiveness, and utilization of training resources.

Timeliness

Reinvented training requires that training professionals rethink the way they have conceived of and delivered training, and that it is no longer acceptable for training to be delivered on a sluggish timetable. Reinvented training is committed to finding ways to bring training more effectively to the customer by providing just-in-time training in a variety of ways that are cost-effective and efficient.

Cost Effectiveness

Reinvented training seeks to find ways to wring more value out of the training budget through radical, revolutionary changes in training delivery and training content. For example, one training function developed several new training approaches to improve efficiency in training resources use by (1) making better use of existing resources through expanding time and equipment allocation; and (2) taking advantage of somewhat inexpensive, readily available technology, such as e-mail, to reach learners.

Flexibility

Reinvented training affects the decision to train through in-house resources, outside contractors, or a combination of the two. In the future, the vendor of choice for specific training will be governed by the results of the performance analysis and needs assessment. Training professionals must acknowledge that for such an assessment to work, in-house training providers must be treated as vendors, meaning that determining how training will be delivered should not be made by the in-house providers. They will become involved only after they have been selected as the vendor.

Means for Evaluation

Reinvented training is committed to providing training so that it can be easily evaluated by its customers. Training functions will have to continue to increase their accountability by creating not only a systems view to the training and development process but also a systematic training evaluation system. The system can be based on Kirkpatrick's (1996) model, a widely used, four-level framework for measuring the effect of training, such as reaction, learning, application, and results. The model depicts identifiable phases of the training process that allow for suitable measures. The four levels build upon one another and collectively form the basis for effective evaluation and decision making. The inclusion of the four-level framework along with a return on investment (ROI), cost-benefit analysis (CBA), and training audit (TA) for measuring the effect of training differs from many traditional efforts where measuring training mainly focused on training design and delivery.

In conclusion, training professionals and their functions who are committed to reinventing themselves must recognize that improvement will be both challenging and rewarding—an adventure, to be sure. An important realization is that training can no longer be independent and microfocused; they must be focused on macrolevel training responsibilities. Thus, improvement requires that training professionals take a fresh approach to relating training to organization performance; the training function must work more closely with the line function and must take a proactive leadership role in helping shape the improvement of the parent organization and in achieving the organization's overall mission. This challenging new role can best be accomplished when the training function is strategic and oriented toward the customer, performance improvement, and accountability.

CONCLUSION

Training is an important function that can contribute directly to an organization's productivity and profitability. The scope of training initiatives vary and include operator, technical, sales, customer service, and various levels of leadership training. Training personnel are involved in needs analysis, design of training initiatives, development of training initiaitves, acquisition of training programs, delivery of training initiatives, and evaluation of training efforts.

As training budgets grow, organizations will expect training efforts to show results. To respond to calls for more accountability and demonstration of the benefits of training, the training function must be committed to continuous change. By constantly looking for ways to reinvent itself and be more responsive to customer demands, the training function will have increased success in contributing to organization and individual success. As the remaining chapters in this book will show, there are a number of traditional and not so traditional things that training professionals can do to further the reinvention of the training process.

CHAPTER 2

Analyzing Training and Development Needs

No single training initiative, much less an entire function, can fulfill its purpose without a needs analysis. Needs analysis identifies the performance areas in which additional training (or nontraining) is needed; it also pinpoints the individuals or groups of employees who could most benefit from the training. In reinvented training, a needs analysis is an important part of a strategic approach to training. Such an approach maximizes the potential success of training efforts.

The purpose of this chapter is to highlight the importance of a strategic approach to training as a natural beginning for training in an organization. The chapter then turns to a more detailed discussion of the importance of the training needs analysis to successful training planning, implementation, and evaluation. Different levels of training needs analysis and methods of collecting information on training needs are reviewed, along with tools that managers and training personnel can use to analyze this information. The chapter will be of particular value in planning, developing, or refining training initiatives by showing that training needs analysis strategies, and the unique organizational characteristics, can and must be blended together to create effective training initiatives tailored to meeting an organization's special needs. Each organization is then in a position to expand the application of training in a dynamic manner to all its employees. The creation of such dynamic training programs can strongly affirm the development and implementation of training initiatives geared toward developing the necessary employee's KSAOCs and attitudes to help the organization achieve its key results.

A STRATEGIC APPROACH TO TRAINING

Today's and tomorrow's training efforts must take place within an overall framework for workforce development that directly contributes to the organization achieving its mission. As Figure 2.1 indicates, such a perspective forms explicit connections between training policies and practices, HR and HRD policies and practices, and the organization's mission and strategic agenda. The premise behind a strategic approach to training is that training decisions that fit the organization's conditions positively impact performance.

A strategic approach to training begins with the relationship between the organization's mission, strategic agenda, and its HRD needs. Current and future HR–workforce requirements are derived from a clear and widely shared understanding of what the organization does and how it does it (including the forward thinking about what the organization needs to do in the future). A strategic approach continues with an assessment of the current capacity of its workforce—what are the composition and core competencies and KSAOCs of current employees? From this assessment, areas of special need and/or continuous upgrading can be identified, and appropriate training (and nontraining) delivered to those in need of it.

But, a strategic approach to training does not conclude here. Organizations must take steps to ensure that the competencies learned and KSAOCs enhanced by training initiatives are indeed applied on the job, and an evaluation system needs to be put in place that can examine the extent to which the competencies and KSAOCs targeted by training do indeed productively advance the mission of the organization. Finally, the organization needs a culture that fundamentally supports ongoing learning as part of the work role of every employee and its own success.

Discussions with most members of an organizations senior leadership would indicate their agreement that such a strategic approach to training is important to an organization's success. However, the real test of their commitment to such an approach is the extent to which they are willing to insist that there be a linkage, or a common thread, between any training, other learning and development initiatives, and the organization. A linkage that consistently stresses the organization's mission, goals, objectives, and strategies can result in a culture of training and learning.

Senior leadership, and a culture that supports ongoing learning and training initiatives, is a key to successful training in any organization. Clearly, improvements in HRD and training in particular will only make a marginal contribution toward increased employee and organizational performance if cultural barriers to sound training reinforce-

Figure 2.1
A Simplified Model of a Strategic Approach to Training

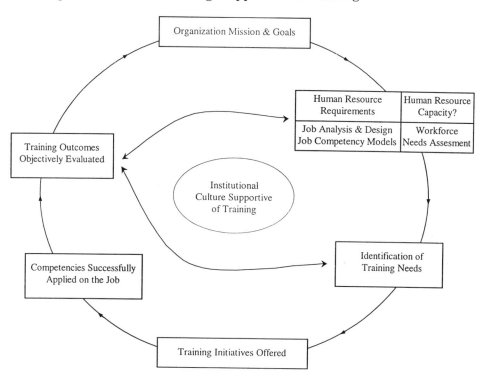

ment exist in the organization. If training is to truly add value to an organization, senior leadership *must* recognize that nothing short of a fundamental reengineering of the training system will enable them to meet the challenges ahead.

Clearly, for training to be successful, it must be inextricably woven into the clarity of the organization's mission, its HR systems, and its culture. All key stakeholders must work towards the development of a strategic plan. One way the organization can begin this process is by stepping back, and working to answer this question: *"If we were designing training from the ground up, today, what would it look like?"*

To do this effectively, a number of issues need to be examined and/or clarified:

1. What are the core areas of human resource capacity that form the heart of the organization's ability to carry out its mission, today? Tomorrow? Within each of these core capacity areas, (a) what are the priorities? and (b) where will the organization get the highest return on its investment, and where will it get the lowest?

2. Where in the organization is it appropriate to locate responsibility for and to commit resources for *each* of these areas?

3. What kinds of alternatives, variations, and flexibilities in substance and delivery systems are required in each of these areas? What obstacles and opportunities currently exist to achieving this flexibility?

4. What training and nontraining resources and delivery systems exist that have yet to be fully tapped?

5. What opportunities exist to address multiple (i.e., across work units) training needs, thus allowing the pooling of training resources across the organization (regionally, nationally, and globally) to be more cost-effective and conserve training dollars? (This is especially viable with the development of so many new technologies for delivering training, which has resulted in increased audience capacity and little additional cost.)

Once the areas of priority for training and nontraining have been confirmed, the organization can embark on a more detailed process to identify or analyze training needs. The remainder of this chapter provides a detailed discussion of training needs analysis.

ROLE OF TRAINING NEEDS ANALYSIS

In today's cost-conscious organizations, the effective analysis of training needs is critical to achieving support for the training intended to improve employee and organizational learning and performance. Needs analysis is the key to designing training programs that create the type of workforce that the organization needs to compete in the marketplace; it also is essential to give employees the KSAOCs they need to successfully complete and compete for jobs within the organization. Without first identifying both organizational and individual learning objectives, training personnel will be hard pressed to prove the ROI needed to justify training funding.

Proactive planning for training must always involve some self-assessment by the training function (for example, by conducting a training audit), looking at future trends that may impact the organization and the training function, determining goals for the function, setting objectives, and developing training plans that are responsive to the current and future training needs of the organization given its strategic agenda. Proactive planning enables the training function to be in a position of helping to make things happen in the organization as opposed to watching things happen. With proactive planning, training personnel view needs analysis as a tool for helping the organization identify problems and opportunities that may be best addressed by either training or nontraining interventions, or a combination of the two. In short, the role of training needs analysis as viewed by proactive training personnel is to work with other members of the organization to ascertain the nature and extent of performance problems or opportunities and potential solutions.

In light of the substantial emphasis placed on training in recent years, it would seem likely that most organizations would have developed extensive methods to identify training needs. Surprisingly, too many organizations still conduct training in a haphazard manner, and too often vast amounts of training dollars are still spent on the "fad of the year" program. The resources wasted on needless or inappropriate training can't help but have backfiring effects on organizations. Money squandered on inappropriate training initiatives are not available for use in other more needy areas of the organization. In addition, employees become frustrated attending programs that prove to be of little value in helping them meet the increasing demands placed on them back on the job, and as one would expect, they become resistant to future training efforts. In order to be effective and worthwhile, training must be driven by an organization's needs. For training to be successful, it requires that needs analysis be continual, that it interface with other organizational areas, and that it incorporate the use of various analyses.

An effective training function cannot develop haphazardly in response to problems as they arise. A strategic (and systematic) approach to developing training efforts requires that some type of needs analysis be conducted to compare the benefits of the efforts with the projected costs and determine the long-term implications of the program. When the need for training is in question or where there could be alternatives, the needs analysis step becomes essential. This step also focuses on the impact of adding to the training and development workload. A well-organized, centralized training function anticipates needs, wards off crises, and eliminates duplication of services.

DETERMINING TRAINING NEEDS

A needs analysis involves collecting information to determine whether a training need exists, and if so, the kind of training required to meet this need. This investigation also should address why the need exists. With this information, organizational leaders and training personnel can identify the KSAOCs to include when designing training initiatives.

HR professionals can conduct the needs analysis using only training personnel, however, the better approach is to develop a task force or resource team that includes both training and nontraining personnel (i.e., line managers, senior leaders, or other employees). Formally involving employees in the needs analysis and design of training initiatives offers several advantages: The training initiatives are more likely to address critical needs, employees will feel more ownership of training programs, and employees and trainers will share greater accountability for fulfilling training objectives.

The first step of the process is to determine the best means for analyzing needs: what levels of analysis should be undertaken, what information to collect, which audience to survey, and what tools to use for collecting and analyzing the data. Analysis of the need for training usually consists of three levels of assessments: organizational, work operations, and employee performance. Training needs might surface in any one of these broad areas.

The Three Levels of Analysis

McGehee and Thayer's (1961) three-level approach to needs analysis has evoked much comment since its inception. Essentially, they considered that training and developmental needs analysis is typically concentrated on the "person" or "task" level, seemingly oblivious to organizational goals. They subsequently described an approach whereby needs analysis at the organization, task, and person level can be integrated to provide an effective training strategy.

First, McGehee and Thayer propose that needs analysis should be undertaken at the organization level to determine where training initiatives should best be directed in the pursuance of organizational objectives. Possibly the most appropriate focus for this area is provided by Katz and Kahn (1978) who suggest that organizational effectiveness can be expressed in the following terms:

- *Goal achievement*, measured in relation to product or service quality, increased output and productivity improvements
- *Increased resourcefulness*, through achievement of greater market share, the establishment of new markets, and increased employee versatility
- *Customer satisfaction*, resulting from the minimization of complaints, the maximizing of on-time deliveries, and an enhanced organizational (or functional) image
- *Internal process improvements*, arising from group cohesion, high standards of supervision, minimal departmental boundaries, and the establishment of realistic and tangible departmental objectives

Consequently the organizational analysis focuses on identifying where within the organization training is needed and examines such broad factors as the organization's culture, mission, strategy, business climate, short- and long-term goals, structure, and the trends likely to affect these objectives. Its purpose is to identify overall organizational needs or opportunities (and the extent to which training is or is not a solution) and the level of support for training. Perhaps the organization lacks the resources needed to support a formal training initiative, or perhaps the organization's strategy emphasizes innovation. In both cases, the organizational analysis that reveals such information plays a major role in determining whether training will be offered and the type of training (or nontraining, or combination of the two) that would be most appropriate. If a lack of resources prevents formal training, an alternative initiative like mentoring or a special project assignment might be used. An environment that focuses on innovation may call for a training initiative that focuses on enhancing employees' creativity.

By definition, training is intended to further the goals of the organization. At a general level, an analysis of training needs must begin with an examination of the organization. Training needs must be analyzed against the backdrop of organizational objectives and strategies. Unless this is done, time and money may well be wasted on training initiatives that do not advance the cause of the company. Employees may be trained in KSAOCs they already possess; the training budget may be squandered on "rest and recuperation" sessions, where employees are entertained but learn little in the way of required KSAOCs and their relationship to achieving important organizational results; or the budget may be spent on glittering hardware that meets the training function's needs but not the organizations.

A thorough needs analysis might look at organizational maintenance, efficiency, and culture. *Organizational maintenance* aims at ensuring a steady supply of KSAOCs. If succession plans point out the need to develop leadership talent, training may include transferring high potential employees through a variety of positions and locations to ensure broad exposure to a variety of responsibilities.

Organizational efficiency might include checking on the degree of goal or results achievement and the extent to which current employees are performing well enough to achieve organizational goals and specific results. There are a number of indicators: productivity, accidents, waste, labor costs, output, quality of product or service, employee performance, or other various organizational measures. Examination of the organization's strategic agenda, the results of HRD planning, and the major variance between the units' successes and failures can help determine the role training could play. The organization's goals and achievement of important expected results can be analyzed for an entire organization, or for an organizational unit such as a department or division. Information on the goals, objectives, and results can be used to identify the scope and content of the training. For example, to meet the goal of increased sales, training in new product knowledge, customer service, and new customer development may be needed.

Organizational culture includes the value system or philosophy of the organization. Like the analysis of efficiency indexes, it can help identify where training initiatives may be needed and provide criteria by which to evaluate the effectiveness of the initiatives that are implemented. Training can be designed to impart the organization's philosophy or values to employees (Argyris 1982).

Analyzing training needs at the organizational level presents problems and future challenges to be met through training. For example, changes in the external environment may present an organization with new challenges. To respond effectively, employees may need training to deal with these changes. The comments of one training manager illustrate the impact of the external environment. "After the American with Disabilities Act in 1990, we had to train every interviewer in the HR department. This training was needed to ensure that our interviewers would not ask questions that might violate federal laws. When managers in other departments heard of the training, they too wanted to sign up. We decided that since they interviewed recruits, they should also be trained. What was to be a one-time seminar became a monthly session for nearly two years."

It is essential to analyze the organization's external environment and internal climate. Trends in the strategic priorities of a business, judicial decisions, civil rights laws, union activity, productivity, turnover, absenteeism, and on-the-job employee behavior will provide relevant information at this level. The important question then becomes, Will training produce changes in employee behavior that will contribute to the achievement of the organization's goals?

In summary, the critical first step is to relate training needs to the achievement of organizational goals. If those responsible for training cannot make that connection, the training is probably unnecessary. However, if a training need does surface at the organizational level, a *work operations analysis* (traditionally referred to as a job or task analysis) is the next step.

Work operations analysis information is a valuable source of data to establish training needs. It requires a careful examination of the work to be performed after training. It involves (1) a systematic collection of information that describes *how* work can be determined; (2) descriptions of how tasks are to be performed to meet the standards; and (3) the KSAOCs and competencies necessary for effective task performance. Job analyses, performance appraisals, interviews (with jobholders, supervisors, and senior leadership), and analysis of operating problems (quality reports and customer reports) all provide important input to the analysis of training needs.

Because the organizational needs analysis is too broad to spot detailed training needs for specific jobs, conducting job analyses during the work operations analysis is essential. Several approaches to analyzing jobs identify training needs. Task analysis, work sampling, critical incident analysis, and task inventories in which employees indicate how frequently they carry out a particular activity and the importance of each activity to the job are all ways to analyze the training needs of a particular job. Job analysis is an examination of the job to be performed. It focuses on the duties and tasks of jobs throughout the organization to determine which jobs require training given the organization's strategic agenda and expected business results. Job analysis requires a careful examination of the job to be performed after training.

A recent and carefully conducted job analysis during the work operations analysis should provide all the information needed to understand job requirements and their expected contribution to achieving specific business results. These duties and tasks are then used to identify the KSAOCs and competency levels required to perform the job adequately. This information is then used to determine the kinds of training needed for the job.

Employee performance analysis determines which employees need training by examining how well employees are carrying out the tasks that make up their jobs (Goldstein 1986; McGehee and Thayer 1961) and can be accomplished in two different ways. Employee performance deficiencies may be identified either by comparing actual performance with the minimum acceptable standards of performance or by comparing an evaluation of employee proficiency on each required KSAOC dimension with the proficiency level required for each skill or area. Performance standards identified in the job analysis phase constitute desired performance. Training is often necessary when there is a discrepancy between an employee's performance and the organization's expectations or standards.

Often, an employee performance analysis entails examining worker performance ratings, then identifying individual employees or groups of employees who are weak in certain KSAOCs. Employee performance data, diagnostic ratings of employees by their supervisors, interviews, or tests (job knowledge, work sample, or situational) can provide information on *actual* performance against which each employee can be compared to *desired* job performance standards. Most often the source of performance ratings is the supervisor, but a more complete picture of workers' strengths and weaknesses may be obtained by expanding the sources to include self-assessment by the individual employee and performance assessments by the employees' peers (Mirabile 1991).

Performance problems can come from numerous sources, many of which would not be affected by training. The only source of a performance problem that training can address is a deficiency that is under the trainee's control (Mager & Pipe 1984). Because training focuses on changing the employee, it can improve performance only when the worker is the source of a performance deficiency. For example, sales training will improve sales only if poor sales techniques are the sources of the problem. If declining sales are due to a poor product, high prices, or a faltering economy, sales training is not going to help.

It is important to note that when we talk about the employee as the source of performance problems, we are not referring only to deficiencies in such hard areas as KSAOCs directly connected to the job. Sometimes the deficiencies occur in such soft areas as diversity and ethics, and they too require training to correct. In any case, a gap between actual and desired performance may be filled by training or nontraining, but a thorough needs analysis helps determine what kind of needs exist.

Training personnel must recognize that analyzing the needs for training does not end here. It is important to analyze needs regularly and at all three levels in order to evaluate the results of training and to assess what training is needed in the future. At the organizational level, training personnel must be proactive in working with senior executives who set the organization's goals, strategies, performance expectations, and who determine and analyze the accompanying training needs. At the work operations level, training personnel must also be proactive in working with the leaders (or teams) who specify how the organization's goals and strategies are going to be achieved and important training needs. At the employee level, training personnel must partner with the leaders and employees who do the work to achieve those goals and strategies and to analyze important training needs, while keeping in mind that performance is a function both of ability and motivation.

METHODS OF COLLECTING AND ANALYZING TRAINING NEEDS DATA

To evaluate the results of training and to assess what training is needed in the future, needs must be analyzed by utilizing the methods of gathering needs analysis data. Training personnel can choose from a variety of specific and different methods for conducting the needs analysis. The more common techniques include: advisory committees, assessment centers, attitude surveys, group discussions, employee interviews, exit interviews, management requests, observations of behavior, performance appraisals, performance documents, questionnaires, and skills test. While the organizational, work operations, and employee performance needs analysis are all important, focusing on the employee's needs as determined by the organization's strategic agenda is especially important. It is at the employee or group level that training is conducted.

There are four ways to determine the employee training needs:

1. Directly observe employees in their actual or future work settings.
2. Interview employees to see what they have to say about their job, performance problems, opportunities, and solutions.
3. Ask supervisors, coworkers, and customers about employees' training needs.
4. Examine the problems or opportunities employees have given the organization's strategic agenda.

In essence, any gaps between the expected and actual performance, results and potential opportunities should suggest training and nontraining needs. Active solicitation of suggestions from the people who know the most about the relative importance of practices, competencies, and the KSAOCs and attitudes important to achieving specific results serves as the best way of determining training needs. Employees themselves, coworkers, supervisors, managers, senior executives, and training oversight committees all can provide valuable information on critical success factors and accompanying training needs.

Regardless of the methods used to collect data during the needs analysis, training personnel will want the information to be reliable—or in other words, to reflect the real work situation. Collecting data from multiple sources is one way of increasing the reliability of the information gathered during a needs analysis.

In deciding on a data collection method, training and development personnel should consider the following criteria (adapted from Robinson & Robinson 1995):

1. The type of data desired (e.g., Do you and your clients want descriptive data that describe the problem or opportunities in narrative terms, or do you want quantified data that provide numerical information?).
2. The size and location of the groups from which data will be collected.
3. The resources available for data collection, including how many people are available to collect data.
4. The potential constraints to collecting the data, including reasons for each constraint.
5. The cost and available funds for collecting data.
6. The amount of time available to collect data.

Data collection methods include one-on-one interviews (either face to face or on the telephone), focus group interviews, questionnaires or surveys, direct observation, and documentation review (the review of organizational documents). The one-on-one interview, focus group interview, and direct observation are most frequently used to collect descriptive data, such as the information used to describe specific performance problems or opportunities. Questionnaires can be quite useful in collecting data for the following reasons: They are well suited for collecting quantifiable data, they allow easy computer tabulation of quantifiable data, they can reach a small or large number of people, they ensure the confidentiality of the respondent, they are familiar to respondents who will tend to respond candidly, they present all questions in a consistent manner to respondents, and they cost less than other data collection methods. Training personnel should use at a minimum two methods for collecting data.

The following sections discuss in more detail various ways of collecting data and the advantages and disadvantages of each approach.

Reviewing Organizational Documents

Organizational documents like HR and other types of records can provide clues regarding performance problems, opportunities and training issues. Advantages of this method are that records provide objective data to identify trouble spots and document performance problems. Disadvantages of this method are that reviewing records can take a long time and may reveal more about past than present situations. Even when the records do reflect current problems, they very seldom indicate causes or possible solutions. Different types of records to check include the following.

Productivity, Sales, and Cost Records

Low productivity and wasted time or materials may indicate a need for cost-control or specific skills training. Declining sales figures can stem from poor customer service or low product quality. By checking customer complaints, training personnel can determine whether the same problems—either with quality control or with customer service—keep coming up. If so, perhaps a refresher or upgrading course is needed for employees in these jobs.

Employee Performance Evaluations and Merit Ratings

Performance evaluations, along with job descriptions, record the KSAOCs required for each job (and class of jobs) and how well current employees are doing given the organization's expected business results. Merit-rating forms also can reveal particular areas where employees slip and might benefit from additional training.

Accident and Safety Reports

Excessive safety problems or accidents problems usually result from inadequate training. If problems tend to cluster in certain departments or certain jobs, employees could benefit from a starter or refresher course in safety training.

Employee Attendance Records

High absenteeism and tardiness can occur when employees feel inadequate in their positions and need further training. Or these problems may arise when a department manager needs more training in how to lead or take on a new role as a team leader when he or she has historically been used to supervising individual employees.

Employee Grievance Filings and Turnover Rates

Employee grievances often reflect problems with either the employee, the immediate supervisor, or the work environment. High turnover can result when employees feel that they are unable to successfully perform their jobs because their skills need upgrading. Training and personnel should talk with managers and check trainee turnover with an eye toward the following factors: Do the new employees leave during their training periods? Do they tend to stay through training, but quit soon after they make the transition to the actual work? If either of these conditions is present, the problem may be solved through training or nontraining interventions.

Conducting One-on-One Interviews

Interviews regarding training needs can be done in person or by phone, formally or informally. Advantages of this method are that interviews can reveal feelings, opinions, and unexpected information or suggestions, including potential solutions to problems and potential opportunities. Disadvantages of using this technique include the time and labor involved in conducting interviews. In addition, good results depend on an unbiased interviewer who listens well and does not judge, interrupt, or distort responses.

Persons to consider interviewing for information on training needs include the following individuals.

Affirmative Action Officers

An organization's plans to increase the employment of minorities and women or to improve the promotability of those already employed create possible training needs for these targeted groups. In addition, affirmative action plans could generate a demand for diversity training for coworkers or supervisors. Also, plans to downsize the organization create problems and opportunities that may have an impact on these targeted groups.

Employment Recruiters

Recruiters are in a position to offer useful information on the KSAOCs of new employees and the changing expectations of new employees as related to training and development opportunities when compared to competitors. If recruiters are having trouble filling particular jobs because of a scarcity of qualified applicants, on-the-job training of current employees or a remedial course for new hires can remedy the situation. If hiring managers routinely administer pre-employment tests for particular positions, test results could point to common areas of weakness among new hires.

Senior Executives

Because senior executives establish the organization's strategic agenda, they can provide the information needed to meet changing circumstances. Training personnel should ask, for example, whether future plans call for any expansion or changes in operations that may alter the organization's HR and HRD needs.

Low and Midlevel Managers

First-line managers and department heads are directly responsible for operationalizing the organization's strategic agenda and performance in their areas. They know what their employees need to learn to improve their present performance and meet future goals. Training personnel should hold regular meetings with low and midlevel managers to keep abreast of and help identify solutions to address changes in their needs.

Conducting Focus Group Interviews

Focus group meetings resemble face-to-face interviews in many ways. Unlike individual interviews, however, focus groups involve simultaneously questioning a number of individuals about training needs.

The number of focus groups to use depends on the number of different work groups with unique training demands. Focus group sessions are more valuable when participants have similar work processes, work closely with each other, or face common situations, such as working with external customers.

Advantages of this method are that focus groups tap many sources and supply qualitative information often omitted when using other inclusive data collection methods, like written questionnaires. Focus groups also can build support for training program proposals and develop participants' problem analysis skills for future feedback. Disadvantages include the time needed to conduct focus groups and the possibility that the group leader may sway the direction of the discussion. In addition, good results depend on group members' ability and willingness to attend and participate in meetings.

Conducting Direct Observations

Direct observation is appropriate to use when the population or the random sample is relatively small, and it is important to note deviations from required procedures. Direct observations can examine on-the-job performance, simulations of work settings, or written work samples. In a small organization, training personnel may be able to pinpoint areas where training is needed simply by watching how jobs are done in various departments. Whatever method is used, training personnel must be sure to talk to employees—they know better than anyone what will help them to improve their job performance.

Advantages of this method are that observations provide a reality check and generate fairly accurate data on performance and work flows with minimal disruption. Disadvantages of conducting observations are that this method is labor-intensive, requires a highly skilled observer, and can be seen as spying.

Using Surveys or Questionnaires

As suggested earlier surveys and questionnaires generally use a standardized format for gathering information. Common survey methods include polling and other forms of questioning, all of which can be administered by mail, phone, or hand.

Advantages of this technique are that surveys and questionnaires cost little, are easy to administer and tabulate, can reach many people in a short time, ensure confidentiality, and identify the scope of a problem. Disadvantages of using surveys include the time and difficulty of constructing clear and unambiguous questions. In addition, written surveys tend to deter individuals from freely expressing their views, which can sacrifice some of the detail and qualitative information gathered using other methods. Surveys also tend to do a better job of identifying problems than pinpointing causes or possible solutions.

Sampling

Sampling is an abbreviated form of surveying. Instead of polling all employees, sampling surveys a small, selected group of employees.

Advantages of sampling are that it is less time-consuming than a regular survey and can target the most important users of training. Disadvantages of sampling are that inappropriate sample selection can bias the results, and the uniqueness of the sample may make it difficult to compare training survey results from year to year.

Administering Group Tests

Testing a group of potential training participants can identify which employees could most benefit from training. It also can highlight weak areas of KSAOCs that the training initiative should target.

Advantages of using tests are that testing quantifies knowledge and ability levels and provides useful "before" data for later use in evaluating the effectiveness of the training. Disadvantages of tests are that many measure only knowledge, not actual job performance, and designing tests that accurately measure the right knowledge or skill can prove difficult.

RECORDING NEEDS ANALYSIS INFORMATION

Along with particular methods for collecting and analyzing needs analysis information, there are a number of tools available to training personnel for recording information. These tools are briefly discussed in the following sections.

Chart or Check Sheets

Organizations can use a chart or check sheet to monitor the training needs of an individual employee. A suggested chart has seven columns: employee, task, nature of training needed, completion date of training, performance level desired, performance level attained, and date of assessment. This chart should keep track of performance weaknesses, training efforts undertaken, and the performance improvement targeted and performance level attained as a result of the training undertaken. The information on the chart indicates the managers' assessment of training needs and return on investment in terms of job performance. The chart can be used for newcomers without KSAOCs needed for a job, employees performing marginally due to skill deficiency, and employees whose job has or will significantly change.

Check sheets can use simple hash marks to record how often certain events occur. This type of information often is charted as a frequency graph that shows the relative severity of different problems. To construct a check sheet, training personnel should take the following steps:

(1) decide exactly what events to record; (2) determine the time period for data collection (hours, days, or possibly months); (3) design a clear and easy-to-use form for recording events; and (4) record events using a consistent format and random observations.

Line Graphs

A line graph visually represents trends in a particular activity over a specified time period. By tracking a particular activity (e.g., on-time delivery or productivity), line graphs to help to identify changes as soon as they occur, allowing prompt attention to problems.

Line graphs can display occurrences of a particular activity, as well as average trends over time. Averages are useful for monitoring future activity to determine if a change is significant enough to cause concern. A change of six or more points from the average is usually worth investigating.

Pareto Charts

A Pareto chart is a bar chart that shows the relative importance of different events. The most frequent events are charted on the far left, with other data recorded in descending order to the right. Like a check sheet, a Pareto chart identifies root causes of problems.

TRANSLATING NEEDS ANALYSIS INFORMATION INTO TRAINING NEEDS

Once an organization has gathered needs analysis data, the next step is to analyze the information to identify training and nontraining needs common to the organization, several departments, or groups of employees. Typical triggers for training include performance problems, poor communication skills, technological advances, or strategic initiatives, such as a move toward quality management or diversification.

When examining needs analysis information, training personnel must be sure to distinguish between actual training needs and isolated problems. Some problems common to several employees may best be addressed through other HR programs, such as the performance management system or employee disciplinary policy. Consideration should also be given to ways in which a shared problem may require different training solutions. For example, a communication problem may exist throughout the organization, but the underlying cause might involve interpersonal or human relations skills training in one department, managerial training in another department, and so on.

Identifying Training and Development Objectives

After completing the three types of analyses in the needs analysis, the training personnel should begin to develop program or learning objectives for the various performance discrepancies. Learning objectives describe the performance you want learners to exhibit. Well-written learning objectives should contain observable actions (e.g., time on target, error rate for things that can be identified, ordered, or chartered), measurable criteria (e.g., percentage correct), and the conditions of performance (e.g., specifications as to when the behavior should occur) (Bernardin & Russell 1998).

Though training objectives can be developed without deriving learning objectives, there are several advantages to developing them. First, the process of defining learning objectives helps the training professional identify criteria for evaluating the initiative. For example, specifying a learning objective of a 20-percent reduction in waste reveals that measures of waste may be important indicators of program effectiveness. Second, learning objectives direct training personnel to the specific issues and content to focus on. This ensures that the training personnel are addressing important topics that have been identified through strategic HR–HRD planning. Also, learning objectives guide learners by specifying what is expected of them at the end of various initiatives. Finally, specifying objectives makes those responsible for training more accountable and more clearly linked to HR planning and other HR activities, which may make the initiatives easier to sell to line managers.

In the end, regardless of the methods used to collect needs analysis information, the success of needs analysis is dependent upon organizational support, and training personnel must ensure that such support exists from each level of the organization.

Gaining Support for the Needs Analysis

Flawed needs analysis processes, a lack of organizational support for needs analyses, and inadequate training personnel expertise are common problems that can undermine the needs analysis and the initiatives built upon its results. Some solutions for countering these problems when conducting a needs analysis are as follows.

First, make sure that you have developed rigorous and thorough procedures for gathering information on training needs. Besides increasing the variety of sources used, the needs analysis process should target specific areas of inquiry. In particular, training personnel should ask for the following information: details of optimal performance; details of actual performance; feelings of employees, supervisors, experts, and others; and causes of problems paired with training and nontraining recommendations and solutions.

Next, training personnel should seek to create organizational support for the needs analysis process. (Seeking such support can be unnecessary if the training personnel have effectively partnered with clients who take the lead on getting and maintaining organizational support for the needs analysis.) Recommended ways to achieve this objective include the following: Document the needs analysis and the way it contributes to the bottom line. (How does the needs analysis contribute to streamlining the training initiative? How does it help identify policy changes that diminished the need for training? How has it shown that a new leadership training or development initiative would enhance the transfer of skills back to the job?) Make a case for needs analysis through analogies to other functions in the organization. (Would a manufacturing department introduce a new product without testing it first?) Finally, increase the expertise of those responsible for completing needs analysis projects. Training personnel should watch out for a needs analysis process that has no expert, as well as one that has indecisive or conflicting experts.

DECIDING WHETHER TO MAKE OR BUY TRAINING

Once an organization has developed a clear picture of its training needs, the next step is to decide the best way to meet these needs. For most organizations, this decision involves several "make-or-buy" issues about both the design and the delivery of the training initiatives. The organization can develop and deliver training initiatives in-house; it can hire an outside consultant to design the initiatives for in-house delivery; it can contract with an outside training facility to handle all aspects of the training; or it can purchase a commercially marketed training initiative and train in-house staff to teach this initiative. Organizations without in-house training functions usually look outside the organization for all but the most basic types of on-the-job training initiatives. For organizations that do have internal training personnel, the decision is more complex. Asking the following questions can help narrow the choice:

- *How often and to how many employees will the training initiative be offered?* If the training initiative addresses a one-time need, targets only a few employees, or will take place only a few times a year, using an outside consultant may prove more cost-effective. On the other hand, ongoing training routinely needed by large numbers of employees can be cheaper when developed and delivered in-house.

- *Will the training involve generic KSAOCs or a specific technical need?* When training involves technology, equipment, or KSAOCs unique to the company and its jobs, in-house design and delivery may be the only option. But for other types of training, commercial vendors offer many programs ranging from functional literacy skills, to desktop publishing software, to managerial development.
- *Will the participants be lower-level employees or upper-level managers?* For top management, a consultant's polished presentation and broad range of experience with other executives and organizations enhances the initiative's credibility. For lower-level positions, participants may view a program as more relevant and credible if it is developed and delivered by someone familiar with day-to-day problems.
- *Will the content of the initiative involve proprietary or competitive information?* If so, the organization may want to develop and deliver the training itself rather than risk trusting an outside consultant with this type of information.
- *How urgently is the training needed?* If the training is essential for meeting some deadline, sometimes an outside vendor or consultant can deliver the training in less time than it would take in-house staff to design and implement an initiative from scratch.

Once the organization has made the make or buy decision, they are then ready to move further into the training design and implementation process. For organizations that decide to do their training in-house, they must determine the types of training methods to use to address the needs identified during the needs analysis. Types of training methods are discussed in the next chapter.

CONCLUSION

The first major step in planning and developing training initiatives is to determine the need for such efforts within an organization. Any training must be linked directly to an organization's strategy, and to employee training and nontraining needed to bring the strategy to fruition. Without such a link, there is no objective basis on which to determine the need for training versus nontraining in an organization or to budget or even estimate costs and benefits. Indeed, when training is seen as peripheral to the real work of the organization, there is little rationale for conducting or supporting training efforts.

When a training needs analysis grows directly out of the organization's strategy, then training becomes for practical purposes very vital to the success of an organization, which, in fact, it always should be. Deriving training needs from the organization's strategy or overall plan may not provide automatic answers to training needs, but it at least starts at the right place.

There are three specific levels of analysis (organization, work operations, and employee performance) that training personnel should use when conducting needs analysis. There are also a number of tools available to record the information collected from the needs analysis. Chart or check sheets, line graphs, and Pareto charts all make the job of collecting needs analysis information easier for training personnel.

Gaining support for training is important to the success of training. Such support is more likely when training personnel have completed a thorough needs analysis that has included input from managers and identifies both training and nontraining needs. Finally, the organization must determine whether it wants to respond to training needs identified during the needs analysis through internal or external sources or a combination of both. In either case, those responsible for training can be assured that the likelihood of training having an impact is increased when the needs analysis was completed before moving forward in the training process.

CHAPTER 3

Designing Effective Training and Development Initiatives

Those responsible for training must constantly delve deeply into the nature of what is competent employee performance in jobs given their organization's strategic agenda, and then relate it to the design of training initiatives. The work of the occasional insightful training professional has shown concern with how complex and diverse KSAOCs are learned and developed. Designing training initiatives which develop important KSOACs is the most challenging aspect of a trainer's role. With the vast increase in knowledge, technology, and complexity in organizations, the training professional must respond to constant demands for training initiatives that result in employees who can perform at expected organizational levels.

After a needs analysis has been conducted (and the make or buy decision made) those responsible for training should be confident that training is needed to address employee problems or needs and to advance the organization's mission. If training *is* the solution, then training initiatives are developed. This can be done by in-house personnel or by outside consultants. Many organizations now even design and manage their own corporate training and development centers. Some of them include Disney, General Electric, Home Depot, Motorola, and Kodak. To develop the training initiatives, the training professional must ensure that they design initiatives conducive to learning. This can be done by setting preconditions for learning and arranging the training environment to ensure learning. Following this, the training person should examine various training methods and techniques to choose the combination most beneficial for accomplishing the learning objectives of the initiatives.

This is the first of two chapters that highlight the importance of design to the overall success of training efforts. After briefly discussing principles of learning important to the effective design of training initiatives, this chapter highlights the importance of identifying pivotal KSAOCs. Next, a tried and tested experiential learning model (ELM) that can be used to enhance the design of initiatives and facilitate participant's learning is discussed. The chapter concludes with a discussion on principles derived from the ELM that can enhance the design of initiatives important to learning pivotal KSAOCs. The next chapter will provide a more detailed examination of various training methods and techniques to complete our discussion of the design phase of training initiatives.

PRINCIPLES OF LEARNING

Well-designed training initiatives facilitate the learning, development, and professional growth of an organization's workforce. And because implementation of such initiatives can be viewed as an investment in human resources, employee morale is likely to improve as employees see themselves as valuable members of the organization. Such a situation will likely result in higher levels of employee performance, achievement of key organizational goals, and increased productivity.

Thorough organizational, work operations (job or task), and employee performance analyses that define the KSAOCs and required competency levels of various positions within an organization provide the information needed to accurately assess both an employee and an organization's training needs. Such assessments aid in the design of effective, viable training initiatives. Once designed, the implementation of initiatives is in the hands of the those who will be actually conducting the training.

To promote efficient learning, long-term retention, and application of the KSAOCs learned during training, findings regarding principles of learning can be helpful in the design of both formal and informal training initiatives. The following is a brief summary of the way learning principles can be applied to training efforts (Hilgard & Bower 1996).

The trainee must be motivated to learn. In order to learn, a person must want to learn. In the context of training, motivation influences a person's enthusiasm for training, keeps attention focused on the training activities, and reinforces what is learned. Motivation is influenced by the beliefs and perceptions of the participants.

The trainee must be able to learn. To learn complex things, a person must have certain aptitudes. The ability to learn to play a role in what is taught in a training effort can be understood and applied back at work.

The learning must be reinforced. Researchers have demonstrated that people learn best with fairly immediate reinforcement of appropriate behavior. The learner must be rewarded for new behavior in ways that satisfy needs, such as pay, recognition, and promotion. Standards of performance should be set for the learner. Benchmarks for learning provide goals and give a feeling of accomplishment when reached. These standards provide a measure for meaningful feedback.

The training must provide for practice of the material. Time is required to assimilate what has been learned, to accept it, to internalize it, and to build confidence in it. This requires practice and repetition of the material.

The material presented must be meaningful. Appropriate materials for sequenced learning (i.e., cases, problems, discussion outlines, or reading lists) must be provided. The trainer acts as an aid in an efficient learning process.

The learning methods used should be as varied as possible. In most learning situations it is boredom that destroys learning, not fatigue. Any method—whether an old-fashioned lecture, programmed learning, or a challenging computer simulation—will begin to bore some learners if overused.

The material must be communicated effectively. Communication must be done in a unified way and over enough time to allow absorption.

The material taught must transfer to the job. The trainer must do her or his best to make the training as close to the reality of the job as possible. Thus, when the participant returns to the job, the training can be applied immediately.

Training professionals should regularly review the basic principles of how individuals learn. This is done in order to set up effective preconditions for learning and a learning environment where learners will be prepared for the training initiatives. Learning principles should be integrated into the design of all training initiatives and materials. Also, issues of how to maximize the transfer of learning of new behaviors back to the job should be addressed. Finally, training professionals should design initiatives to meet the needs of adults as learners, which means understanding how adults learn best.

DESIGNING FOR LEARNING AND DEVELOPMENT OF PIVOTAL KSAOCS

A number of training initiative designs and instructional strategies have been proposed and described in the training literature in the last twenty-five years. Each of these designs and methods were intended to increase the effectiveness of employee learning. While evidence does show that variables such as organization and presentation of material can induce a difference in participant's learning, each training design must relate to a greater goal: training (and development) focused on KSAOCs critical to achievement of business results. The challenge for today's training function is to design initiatives that improve each employee's ability to achieve the results he or she must produce. This is not a revolutionary idea. Peter Drucker, the man who literally wrote the book on results, made the point twenty-five years ago: "If you want to know, What development do I need? ask first, What results are expected of me?" (Murphy 1997). By ensuring that *all* training efforts are driven by a clear understanding of the results expected of the organization and its employees when designing learning activities, training personnel can best be assured that they are focusing on the needs of their customers.

A results and customer-satisfaction strategy is important to the success of any training initiative. This focus is achieved by designing programs that develop KSAOCs identified as critical or pivotal (versus peripheral) to achievement of important business results. As noted in Chapter 2, a prerequisite to designing training initiatives critical to achieving organizational and individual results is an ongoing needs analysis process. When the training initiatives are the direct results of needs analysis, training designers know exactly what KSAOCs and accompanying competency levels are pivotal to addressing an organizational problem, need, or opportunity.

Pivotal KSAOCs are not only central but necessary for successful completion of jobs important to achievement of organizational goals. Peripheral KSAOCs refer to KSAOCs that an employee may possess, but that have no extraordinary or perhaps even significant impact on the level of performance on the job. Thus, training initiative designs must emphasize proficiency and competency in pivotal KSAOCs of various jobs.

The Importance of Training for Competence

The responsibility associated with designing programs that focus on learning and successfully applying pivotal KSAOCs and competency levels cannot be understated. Inadequate design or implementation of efforts not tailored to an organization's problems, needs, or opportunities can often lead to capital losses and competition.

While the design of effective training initiatives is an integral part of implementing successful training, the design is of little consequence unless the content of such efforts appropriately corresponds to the organization's needs and goals. Thus, initiative designers must determine the very specific qualifications dictated by the various positions within an organization, identify evaluation indicators, and finally, develop a customer-responsive and functional system.

Determining the qualifications or competencies appropriate for a given position involves more than simple identification of the KSAOCs required by that position. Butler defined competence as "the ability to meet or surpass prevailing standards of adequacy for a particular activity" (1978, p. 7). This definition can be expanded to include an individual's values, critical thinking patterns, judgment, and processes of attitude formulation and integration of other learning into performance of one's job. With this in mind, it becomes evident that a well-designed training initiative is one that prepares its participants to successfully apply integrated KSAOCs in a practical and job-related manner. To ensure that the focus of the initiative is on outcome rather than simply on development of KSAOCs and behavior, an evaluation process must be developed during the design phase to measure the extent to which the expected goals have been achieved.

Competence in pivotal KSAOCs is the ability to meet or surpass prevailing standards of performance for a particular activity. It includes job-related behaviors and KSAOCs. Pivotal KSAOC-based training is derived from the identification of pivotal KSAOCs and provides learning and development opportunities designed to develop and enhance those KSAOCs. The evaluation process must measure the extent to which development and enhancement of pivotal KSAOCs have been achieved. All learning and development activities must also focus on outcome and not merely on the acquisition of KSAOCs. Pivotal KSAOC-based training should include the following characteristics:

1. Pivotal KSAOCs must guide planning of all learning and development activities. Each pivotal KSAOC should describe a desired behavioral outcome, and through this description it should guide the planning, the implementation of learning experiences, and the prescription of criterion and methods of evaluation.

2. Pivotal KSAOCs should be derived from roles and emphasize performance rather than just knowledge acquisition. Pivotal KSAOCs emphasize how each participant will use their acquired KSAOCs back at work. Learning these pivotal KSAOCs never ends with simple recall. Each pivotal KSAOC is always stated in such a manner as to answer the question, "How will the participant utilize the pivotal KSAOC back at work?"

3. Pivotal KSAOCs emphasize judgement, not merely psychomotor skill. Pivotal KSAOC development is not simply performing a skill. It includes making some judgment about the accuracy and appropriateness of the use of the KSAOC, and it implies a standard of excellence. The pivotal KSAOC directs and ensures learning in the higher levels of the cognitive, affective, and psychomotor domains.

4. Pivotal KSAOCs state the conditions under which a participant performs, the actions or behaviors, and the standard of performance. An example of a pivotal KSAOC statement is as follows: Based on the principles of orga-

nization strategy, leaders will be able to analyze critically any organization threats, opportunities, strengths, and weaknesses and determine the
applicability of their organization's strategic agenda given said analysis.

Pivotal KSAOCs must be achieved during various training (and
nontraining) efforts. Because pivotal KSAOCs prescribe learning, development, and evaluation, a variety of methods must be incorporated
in the final design of any training initiatives. Efforts toward the design of training initiatives that develop pivotal KSAOCs would be
greatly facilitated by the application of a clear model of pivotal KSAOC-
based and competency level-oriented initiative design. Kolb's (1984)
ELM provides such a framework from which to draw ideas.

It is also important for those responsible for training to understand
that the development of pivotal KSAOCs is dependent upon several
conditions, each of which implies a principle that should be incorporated into the design of the training if pivotal KSAOC development is
to result. These principles will be presented following a discussion of
Kolb's ELM.

KOLB'S EXPERIENTIAL LEARNING MODEL

Once the organization and its employees have been subjected to needs
analyses, and pivotal KSAOCs have been identified, training personnel must then turn to designing initiatives that will result in employees who are more skilled in the performance of their jobs. In the modern
"learning organization," successful design of learning initiatives is the
true test of whether those responsible for training are fulfilling their
assigned charter. The training function must be able when designing
initiatives to positively respond to questions like the following: Are we
designing initiatives that are helping technical, knowledge, and management workers to perform new tasks and replace outdated work
habits? Or are we just showing them stuff and telling them stuff and
making them do stuff, then sending them back to their jobs and hoping
they get better?

Questions like these wouldn't be so bothersome to those in the profession if we could better demonstrate that our training initiatives have any
real effect at all. However, insufficient detail to training design contributes to our difficulty in demonstrating the value of training efforts. Is
there something better training personnel should be doing instead?

The answer is yes! Today the design of too many training initiatives
are still based upon the old content-delivery design assumption: that if
we gather sufficient information (or insight or wisdom) about an
employee's work, and if we artfully disclose that information in their

presence, using lectures or the latest video, then surely, surely, they will go back to work and start performing their work more competently. Unfortunately, training personnel have had little supportive evidence that people depart from our content-disclosure designed sessions with suddenly improved behaviors or KSAOCs, or that they predictably acquire them later.

At the heart of all experiential learning theory lies the fundamental belief that learning occurs when an individual is actively involved with concrete experience (Walters & Marks 1981). Although many terms and definitions are used to describe this particular type of learning (Gentry 1990, 10) a useful definition that emphasizes the full involvement of the learner's intellect, feelings, and behavior was given by Hoover and Whitehead: "Experiential learning exists when a personally responsible participant cognitively, affectively, and behaviorally processes knowledge, skills, and/or attitudes in a learning situation characterized by a high level of active involvement" (1975, p. 25).

While it would be difficult to argue that experience does not lead to some learning, it would be equally difficult to prove that the right sort of learning will occur unless certain conditions exist supporting this learning. The challenge for training personnel who wish to design effective programs is to be sure that they foster learning that enhances an employee's performance and meets organizational goals.

Though there are numerous models and theories of experiential learning, Kolb's ELM is the most popular and most frequently referred to in experiential literature (Henry 1989, 26). Kolb defines experiential learning as a "process whereby knowledge is created through the transformation of experience" (1984, 38). It is this process, not specific outcomes, and the mechanisms that transform experience into knowledge that interest Kolb and are illustrated in his model (see Figure 3.1).

Kolb begins with concrete experience (CE) that motivates the learner to reflect on that experience (RO). Reflection then leads to the testing of existing concepts and the formation of new ones from which learners make sense of their world (AC). Learners then test these concepts by actively experimenting with their world (AE), which begins the cycle once again (CE), but now from a newer perspective modified by what has been learned. The use of the circle in Kolb's model does not accurately capture the upward, spiraling nature of the learning process suggested by his theory. For when learners begin the cycle again, they begin from a higher level of "cognitive functioning" (1984, 23).

Drawing heavily from the works of Kurt Lewin, John Dewey, and Jean Piaget, Kolb depicts the experiential learning process as a continuous interaction between the individual and the world. Indeed, Kolb describes it as a "tension- and conflict-filled process" as the individual attempts to adapt to the world and integrate its experiences into new states of knowing and behaving. To be successful, the learner must struggle to resolve such dialectical tensions and conflicts at the cognitive, affective, and behavioral levels, conflicts that require special skills at each stage of his four-part cycle.

Kolb asks, "How can one act and reflect at the same time? How can one be concrete and immediate and still be theoretical?" (1984, 30). The answer, he feels, lies in the types of abilities required of learners, abilities that are polar opposites, such as the ability of abstract conceptualization and its opposite—apprehension and observation; or the ability to adapt primarily by reflection and its opposite—active experimentation. As indicated by the horizontal and vertical arrows in Figure 3.1, there is a tension or pull felt by learners between their active and reflective faculties and between their immediate relation to concrete experience and their ability for formulating concepts. According to Kolb, each stage of learning and each mode of adaptation requires different kinds of abilities, sometimes working in tandem, sometimes working alone; but, any one faculty or mode is insufficient to lead to the sort of holistic learning process that integrates thinking, feeling, perceiving, and behaving (31). Ideally, learners "must be able to get involved fully, openly, and without bias in new experiences (CE), to reflect upon and interpret these experiences from different perspectives (RO), to create concepts that integrate these observations in logically sound theories (AC), and to use these theories to make decisions and solve problems (AE) leading to new experiences" (Kolb & Lewis 1986, 99). What is suggested by Kolb's model is the subtlety and complexity of learning in relation to individual abilities and problem-solving skills.

Kolb's work in this area began with his experimentation with games, exercises, simulations, and case studies. He discovered that his learners had marked preferences for different types of experiential learning activities that reflected certain phases of the experiential learning cycle (Smith & Kolb 1986, 3). This fact led him to his concept of learning styles. Kolb explains individual learning differences in terms of learning styles. One might think of individual learners as having either an innate or learned preference or style for processing experience. Styles, however, are not fixed traits, but rather ways the mind operates (Smith & Kolb 1986, 4). Kolb refers to these styles as underlying structures or "possibility-processing structures" that impact on the learning process (Kolb 1984, 78). The convergent learner, for instance, has the dominant learning abilities of abstract conceptualization and active experimentation. This learner's greatest strength is found in "problem solving, decision making, and the practical application of ideas." Such learners, Kolb feels, are excellent at technical tasks. The divergent learner, on the other hand, approaches experience from an opposite perspec-

Figure 3.1
Kolb's Experiential Learning Model

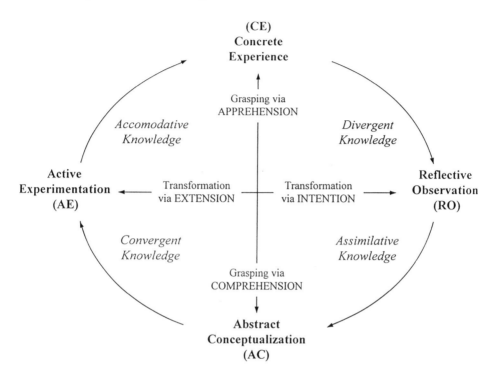

Source: D. A. Kolb, *Experiential Learning*. 1984. Englewood Cliffs, NJ: Prentice Hall.

tive, emphasizing concrete experience and reflective observation. This learner is best at generating alternative ideas and imaginative solutions. This learner is also people-oriented and feels comfortable dealing with people's emotions.

A learner who relies on assimilative faculties is a reflective learner who forms concepts and loves ideas. Such learners gravitate to the theoretical professions and are less concerned with people than ideas. Finally there are learners whose learning styles function best with concrete experience and active experimentation. This learner is a doer, someone who can carry out plans and get involved with new projects. Such a learner adapts best to a changing environment and prefers the trial and error method.

Researchers suggest that learners who rely too much on one type of learning style are ill-equipped to handle and therefore learn from some experiences. An assimilator may end with exquisite theories but with no practical ways for applying them; a converger, with solutions to the wrong problems; a diverger may be paralyzed by the alternatives generated; and the accommodator may produce tremendous ends but all in the wrong area (Packham, Roberts, & Bawden 1989, 138).

Learning styles, Kolb argues, are the result of a combination of heredity, education, experience, and the demands of the environment. Although he concentrates on four main learning styles and suggest that learners lean towards one of the above styles or a combination of them, he is quick to point out that learners may learn the other styles. There is convincing empirical evidence that work preference is strongly correlated with learning styles (see Laschinger & Boss 1984; McCart, Toombs, Lindsay, & Crowe 1985). Like Myers-Briggs, McCarthy, and Honey and Mumford, Kolb has developed a testing instrument that helps learners identify their learning styles. (For studies on the validity of these instruments see Sims, Veres, & Shake 1989; Veres, Sims, & Locklear 1991).

Several aspects of this model are important to note for those designing training initiatives. First, the model shows learning to be more than a stimulus–response process. Thinking and analysis occur during reflection and generalization, as well as in the testing of hypotheses. Second, the learning cycle is continuous. Previous learning influences current learning; and current learning influences future learning in a developmental or training process.

Forgetting can also be explained by this model of learning. Forgetting is caused not merely by the passage of time, but rather by the events that occur after the initial learning experience (Manis 1966). After the learning cycle is completed, an individual begins a new learning cycle. Perhaps the new learning invalidates the old learning, or just consumes the person, not allowing practice of the previously learned behavior. In the design of training efforts, if training personnel expect a person to remember something he or she has just learned, they must allow the person to continue to repeat it (i.e., applying it in a particular work situation), so that forgetting does not occur. It also does not hurt to continue to reward desired behavior. Withholding a reward can cause the extinction of the behavior, which is much like forgetting.

The third point about Kolb's model is that since the learning process is cyclical, it is possible to begin new learning at any stage of the process. For example, a person may read about a new theory of management before going out to experiment with this new information. Here, the person enters at the abstract conceptualization stage and then progresses to the testing hypothesis stage. Where a person starts and the direction his or her learning takes depend on the individual's goals and needs as well as on previous learning and the stage that has been rewarded in the past.

The three preceding points suggest the final point: learning is a highly individualized process. While it is difficult for others to observe, since it is an internal process application of learning to work, situations and problem solving can be observed. People have different styles of learning. Training personnel must be cognizant of the four styles or activities—divergence, assimilation, convergence, and accommodator (the author prefers to use the term "implementation" rather than "accommodation" as used by Kolb because "accommodation" implies passivity and compromise)—when designing training initiatives and how they might use this information in understanding and training employees. For example, should a training effort have people of similar learning styles, or would it be better to have a variety of styles? With a variety of pivotal KSAOCs and competency levels introduced in training initiatives, what combination of styles should be mixed? How can training personnel provide different learning and development opportunities to people with different learning styles?

Capabilities for performing tasks at an appropriate skill level vary according to each individual in each learning and performing stage. Predictable weaknesses are associated with either an excess or a deficiency in any state. Kolb's ELM incorporates the conditions of adult learning into a framework that can be applied to the design of training initiatives which emphasize the development of pivotal KSAOCs and competency levels by participants. Given Kolb's ELM, some principles that are helpful to training personnel when designing training initiatives are discussed in the next section.

ENHANCING PIVOTAL KSAOCs AND COMPETENCY DEVELOPMENT

The development of pivotal KSAOCs and attainment of competency levels by employees that are important to achieving organization results is dependent on several conditions, each of which implies a principle that must be incorporated into the design of training programs. These principles are as follows:

1. *Developing pivotal KSAOCs and attainment of competency levels requires a high tolerance for eclecticism, due to the frequency with which employees face new work situations, opportunities, and problems.* Tolerance for eclecticism—the acceptance of and ability to deal with varying points of view—can be expanded through experience and social support. Given the ever changing demands of the world of work, the prospective employee (learner) needs prototypes to adjust to a wide variety of organizational and work or job settings. Equally important is the learning of pivotal KSAOCs so that the learner will learn to adapt rapidly to the realities of particular work situations. While de-

velopment of a high tolerance for eclecticism may appear easy to acquire at first glance, it is in reality exceedingly difficult to accomplish. This is so because people differ from each other in fundamental ways, and often view the differences in knowledge, ability and skill levels, performance, race, age, education or socioeconomic position, to be good or bad, right or wrong, or appropriate or inappropriate. It is fairly obvious that judgmental dichotomous attitudes are problematic. Even more problematic is the fact that people are different in terms of personality and temperament. As a result of these very fundamental differences, people have different motives, different purposes and aims, different values, different needs, different drives, different impulses, different urges, and different learning styles. These in turn cause people to perceive, cognize, think, conceptualize, understand, believe, and learn differently from each other (Wolfe 1980).

Those who believe they innately "know" that whatever one is, is "correct," or the way people "should be," are quick to find those who differ from themselves to be fundamentally afflicted, flawed, stupid, lazy, bad, sick, or any combination thereof. Fortunately, our tendency to wish those near us to be just as we are is seldom granted; we are all richer for that. People are fundamentally different and designers of training initiatives must constantly be aware of this difference. Training personnel cannot erase the fundamental differences between people, but they *can* develop a high tolerance for people (learners) who are different. That tolerance can grow into respect for their differences, which are then viewed as neither good nor bad but merely as different. When this happens, tolerance has become a training tool, replacing the detriment of intolerance that was earlier in its place. Training personnel, and indeed any individual in an organization who has not developed the pivotal KSAOC of exercising a high degree of tolerance, is decidedly at a disadvantage when compared with trainers and learners who have. In essence, there is a strong need for the presence, and therefore for the learning and development of flexibility and adaptability, in those responsible for designing training initiatives.

2. *The development of pivotal KSAOCs and attainment of competency levels requires an emphasis on both practice and work application.* An emphasis on experiential learning and active practice in training initiatives requires a clear understanding of the organization's strategic agenda and requisite job performance levels in which the learners work. This understanding includes knowledge about the organization's training needs, the internal or external forces that maintain or change them both, and the possibilities for further training.

Assisting trainees in obtaining pivotal KSAOCs and competency levels also requires training initiative designers to prepare learners to understand the importance of and effective use of the pivotal KSAOCs.

These KSAOCs should help the learners to see clearly what their training needs are and what opportunities exist in the future. Training of pivotal KSAOCs and attainment of competency levels should always emphasize the importance of application and designs that are most appropriate to learning. Such a training design allows one the opportunity to practice pivotal KSAOCs in actual work situations, or in those that are as close as possible to the work environment back home.

3. *Direct experience in settings similar to those in which the learner will perform following their involvement in the training initiative is necessary for the development of pivotal KSAOCs and attainment of competency levels.*

The attainment of pivotal KSAOCs and competency levels comes in part from a cognitive understanding of the role, but primarily from practice—through performing skills, making a critique of the consequences (intended and otherwise) of performance, and exploring and understanding other ways of performing. Active experimentation, observation, and reflection are all necessary components of pivotal KSAOC and competency development. Therefore, learners need to identify and understand the objectives of particular organizational roles, methods, and pivotal KSAOCs. In addition, they need to know which situations call for particular pivotal KSAOCs and the required competency levels, and under what conditions these KSAOCs have the best likelihood of producing desired results. In fact, the learners must understand how these KSAOCs produce any results at all. In short, those responsible for designing training must understand that there are analytical or diagnostic tasks involved in learning different pivotal KSAOCs.

Prospective learners also learn pivotal KSAOCs by seeing them performed and by watching skilled personnel as they demonstrate their work. As an apprentice learns alongside the master craftsman, so too must learners observe others in action and talk with them about their work. The greater the number of exposures to role models, the better the chance that trainees will understand and acquire pivotal KSAOCs and the requisite competency levels. Whether in real work situations or simulations, learners need to try out the particular KSAOCs involved in producing desired results. Learners also need to engage with others in a working capacity—responding to expectations, handling problems, and facing the consequences. The use of experiential learning exercises (ELEs) and the case study method is one way of representing such real work situations and enhancing transfer of learning.

4. *The development of pivotal KSAOCs and appropriate competency levels requires assessment using valid, reliable techniques that measure the impact of training, pivotal KSAOC outputs, and competency levels.* The assessment of competence in pivotal KSAOCs takes place in a context. Usual testing or assessment procedures and contexts as-

sess participants in situations unlike those experienced in a true or actual work environment. Training personnel must not just focus on those learners highly competent at performing a task during a training initiative, yet do not know what to do when confronted with real work problems. In the design of some training initiatives, the learning and development of pivotal KSAOCs by learners does not occur during the initiative because the effort emphasized the wrong setting or context for demonstrating their competencies. According to Wolfe, "However objective and controlled typical assessment procedures are, their validity for measuring competence is in doubt" (1980, 8). Relevant assessments (or the data for them) must be generated in a variety of experiential settings, such as experiences or in situations that closely simulate the work setting back home. The assessment center approach (Moses & Byham 1977; Peterson & Stakenas 1981), which includes written tests as well as techniques such as in-basket exercises and simulations, appears to be a promising way to measure performance in a more suitable context.

Peterson and Stakenas (1981) state the following important characteristics of assessment procedures which would be appropriate for inclusion in the design of training initiatives and measurement of pivotal KSAOCs and competency levels learned: They should call for the integration of subskills into "generic" skills; they should take place in real life or simulated real life settings to enhance the predictability of the behavior occurring in subsequent adult (job) roles in society; they should be technically sound and practical to use; and they should specify generic skills, their subskills, and content.

5. *The development of pivotal KSAOCs and attainment of competency levels require useful feedback.* During the design and implementation of training initiatives training personnel must ensure the availability of feedback about the impact of learner performance. Training personnel face a dilemma: as those often responsible for the training initiatives, they must encourage the realization of full potential, and as evaluators, they must hold learners to high standards of excellence and give valid feedback about the adequacy of performance. An important factor of training and performance initiative design is the creation of a genuine feedback process. For purposes of learning and successful transfer of learning to the back-home situation, feedback is required frequently and soon after performance. More importantly, it must be *descriptive* of the consequences of performance, and not *evaluative* in tone. Direct attention to the development of genuine feedback processes is essential, and learners and training personnel alike need to be clear when the process is feedback and when it is assessment for organizational decisions (i.e., raises, performance appraisals, promotions, and opportunities for future learning and development opportunities).

In addition to trying out acquired methods and pivotal KSAOCs in practical situations, learners must practice critical reflection of the consequences produced by these actions. For our purposes the term "feedback" refers to direct observation of the real consequences of one's act—genuine feedback. Learning progresses much more directly when learners are required to examine and experience. If possible, the results of their decisions receive quick feedback in respect to consequences or probable consequences. This type of feedback allows learners to learn how to detect outcomes and match them against stated objectives. Learners can also decide if the task is finished, or whether they need to do something more, or to accomplish the task by some different means, or even if they must increase their competency, proficiency, or efficiency in order to improve their performance in achieving key business results. Reflecting on genuine feedback stimulates a search for alternative responses, and for what might be more appropriate the next time the problem or situation is encountered. The next cycle of feedback should reinforce improvement and eliminate error or any performance gap.

6. *The development of pivotal KSAOCs and attainment of competency levels is dependent upon increased self-knowledge.* Training personnel must avoid the tendency to treat pivotal KSAOCs and attainment of competency levels as a combination of KSAOCs that can be taught to the learner. Those responsible for designing training must also recognize the special importance of personal growth and self-knowledge. The learner needs to learn to focus inward toward greater self-insight and mastery, as well as outward. Learners must be taught to understand how their needs, expectations, fears, biases, personalities, and learning styles influence their use of pivotal KSAOCs in various work situations. Therefore, one responsibility of those who design training initiatives is to assist learners in understanding that these factors are a part of the pivotal KSAOC development equation, and that they must be identified and understood. A knowledge of self assists learners in realizing what things they can or cannot do, and in developing an identity that integrates KSAOCs, values, propensities, and personal learning strengths. It also provides them with the insight needed to lessen the effects of or to eliminate perceived personal inadequacies (such as weaknesses in certain learning areas) that might impact their ability to achieve expected performance.

7. *Reflection and consolidation are essential final steps in the development of pivotal KSAOCs and attainment of competency levels.* At some point it becomes appropriate to step back, reflect on one's experiences, and consolidate the KSAOCs one has learned. Reflection time is needed for both learners and training personnel to ascertain the acquisition of the KSAOCs that are to be acknowledged through the par-

ticipation in training initiatives and the movement of the learner to higher levels of competency and KSAOC requirements. An assessment or reward for completing the training initiatives, if they are to be meaningful, should be based on learning achievement and successful demonstration of the designated pivotal KSAOCs and attainment of competency levels. It should also provide for learners, training personnel, and organizational leaders a review of the actual pivotal KSAOCs developed, competency levels attained, and any new behaviors. At this point, learners should be prepared to move back to the workplace with the ability to perform well and to further develop pivotal KSAOCs and higher competency levels relevant to their work roles.

RESPONSIBILITIES OF TRAINING PERSONNEL IN INITIATIVE DESIGN

In designing training initiatives that focus on learning pivotal KSAOCs and the attainment of competency levels, the responsibilities of training personnel are much broader than the traditional role of merely imparting knowledge. The tasks facing training personnel in designing training geared to increasing the learning and development of pivotal KSAOCs and the attainment of competency levels are

- identifying the kinds and levels of KSAOCs required for high levels of performance important to achieving organizational results.
- developing and maintaining structures, conditions, and climates conducive to learning.
- generating and providing resources, including their own knowledge of investigative, evaluative, and documentary skills regarding initiative design.
- identifying and providing access to off-the-job as well as on-the-job learning environments and resources.
- providing individual assistance and feedback on various dimensions of the learners' performances in specific pivotal KSAOC areas.
- serving as role models and mentors by guiding and advising organizations and learners as they pursue the mastery of pivotal KSAOCs and achievement of competency levels.
- developing alternative but efficient learning processes that take into account individual learning styles, abilities, and work and life circumstances.

A significant ideological barrier that must be overcome if training initiative designs are to be successfully implemented is the pervasive content orientation of many training personnel. One consequence of this orientation is a preoccupation with the covering of content material, rather than mastering pivotal KSAOCs and achieving competency levels important to the achievement of organizational results. An exclusive preoccupation with knowledge acquisition may foster the implicit (and unwarranted) assumption that such knowledge will "transfer" readily into the KSAOCs needed to meet the demands of life beyond the training initiative. However, in training efforts that emphasize development of pivotal KSAOCs and attainment of competency levels, content is viewed as a means for engendering the capabilities required for survival, excellence, and high levels of performance. This ideological conversion requires thorough consideration of not only ways to train and develop, but how learners are to learn and apply their knowledge in work situations.

In too many training and development situations training personnel have by and large been left to their own devices to determine not only the content to be covered in their courses, but also to determine how well learners are expected to master it. In training efforts that are based on organizational needs analysis and emphasize the learning and development of pivotal KSAOCs and attainment of competency levels, the results of such efforts—namely learning and development in the mastery of pivotal KSAOCs—can be observed and used to evaluate training effectiveness. When training personnel and learners know what is to be learned, they can work together to achieve the required standards.

The kinds of complex KSAOCs required by members of today's organization cannot be developed through only one learning process. Training initiatives based on only one training or learning design will at best make an inadequate contribution to pivotal KSAOC and competency development. Abstract conceptualization (which still tends to be the medium of many training initiatives) is extremely important, but it provides only the first layer of learning. Although the first layer is basic, because it is theoretical in nature, it provides only a concrete foundation upon which specific KSAOCs, the bricks and mortar and thus the visible portion of the training initiative, is built.

The three different learning processes of concrete experience, reflective observation, and abstract conceptualization in combination provide a basis for understanding the problems with which one must deal with in work life. A fourth generic learning process—active experimentation—is a further requirement for the development of pivotal KSAOCs and competency levels. Only when training personnel commit themselves to including these in the design of training initiatives will pivotal KSAOC and competency-based initiatives become more realistic and valued by managers in the organization.

Both the environment and the process of training must be well planned and well managed because of their special contributions to competence. Those aspiring to the higher levels of effective and efficient organizations need to learn how to function effectively in several learning modes and in various environments. Kolb's ELM provides a framework for matching each pivotal KSAOC with the type of training most likely to instill the KSAOCs. As the learner moves through each phase of the model, each KSAOC can be taught using the principles that best facilitate the learning and development of pivotal versus peripheral KSAOCs.

Optimally, the learner and training personnel join in a collaborative venture in which both aspire to a common objective: the development of pivotal KSAOCs and competency in the learner. Both seek and create a wide variety of pivotal KSAOC and competency-based learning experience and both track the course of learning and development. When designers of training initiatives plan and design training initiatives for learners, and when training personnel and learners know what is to be learned, then they can work together to achieve the desired standards as effectively and efficiently as possible.

Learners going through the four phases of Kolb's model are able to test and put into action several different pivotal KSAOCs and competency levels. The first phase of the model aids the learner in identification and articulation of the particular qualifications and characteristics he or she must develop during various training initiatives. It should be remembered that the qualifications to be developed during training initiatives are initially identified and agreed upon through the needs analysis process. The second phase, which involves reflection, focuses on the actual application of what has been learned, and thus enables the learner to develop a clear understanding of what the pivotal KSAOCs and different competency levels actually entail.

Having identified the particular characteristics desired and then reflecting upon their actual application, the learner must then integrate these pivotal KSAOCs into their own conceptual framework in order to test their ideas and impressions against the reality of the work environment. How will the pivotal KSAOCs be applied or used in real work situations? What are the potential alternative reactions or approaches to implementing them?

The fourth phase requires the learner to develop their own implementation (or action) plans. This way, the learner must then identify how the different KSAOCs will be used in the performance of their job back at work. The implementation plan focuses attention on the basic purpose of pivotal KSAOC development and attainment of competency levels in training initiatives: the application or implementation and eventual evaluation of the effectiveness of the pivotal KSAOCs in use. Implementation plans developed by the learner can be stated in the form of rules of thumb or action resolutions, and should be based on the original qualifications identified during Phase I. Again, these are pivotal KSAOCs that can be directly tied to specific jobs, work units, and results.

Kolb's ELM is cyclical. Once a learner integrates new characteristics into their behavioral repertoire, future job performance will require dependence on the enhanced or new competency level achieved. This interaction sometimes involves modification of the use of the different pivotal KSAOCs and becomes the source for new learning needs. Thus, learning is an ongoing process for the learner (and the organization) and is continuously shaped by the requirements of future organizational needs and learning and development initiatives.

CONCLUSION

Successful training in organizations depends on a systematic approach that involves a careful needs analysis, solid program design, and thorough evaluation. Training initiatives should not be designed as quick fixes for every organizational problem, nor should they rely on faddish techniques. Instead, training should be designed to meet the particular needs of the organization and its employees. It should be viewed as a continuous learning endeavor by employees and managers to stay current and to anticipate future needs.

Training professionals can be maximally effective in their design of initiatives that facilitate employee learning by defining clearly what is to be learned before beginning the design process. Defining what is to be learned requires a continuous cycle of analysis of the training needs of employees given the organization's strategic agenda. Then, real training needs can be linked to the achievement of broader organizational goals, ensuring that they are consistent with management's perception of strategy and tactics. Beyond these fundamental concerns, principles of learning are essential considerations in the design of any training initiative.

Training personnel can also make use of Kolb's ELM in developing and designing training initiatives that are driven by organizational problems, opportunities, and needs. The fundamental assumption in the application of Kolb's ELM in designing training initiatives is that learning should be based on experience. Training personnel can use the ELM to design training initiatives that emphasize learning pivotal KSAOCs in specific areas by (1) focusing on work-related problems or situations, (2) by requiring the learner to reflect on the behavior or KSAOCs being learned, (3) by examining possible solutions or alternative approaches for using the KSAOCs, and (4) by constructing a strategy for implementing the KDAOC. The process leads back to Phase I of the model and the cyclical process begins again.

CHAPTER 4

Training and Development Methods

New methods available to those in the training profession appear every year. While some are well founded in learning theory or models of behavior change (e.g., behavior modeling), others result more from technological than theoretical developments (e.g., videotapes, computer-based business games). In either case, trainers have a wide variety of methods, materials, and media from which to choose in designing and delivering training initiatives. Which training techniques best suit a particular initiative depends on the learning objectives and cost considerations. Most training initiatives use multiple methods and training aids.

While the previous chapter focused on the design of training efforts, this chapter looks at different training methods available to training professionals. In addition to highlighting some of the strengths and weaknesses of the different methods, this chapter discusses criteria important in choosing the method or combination of methods to use during training.

TYPES OF TRAINING METHODS

Once the needs analysis has been completed and training goals and objectives have been established, decisions must be made on the training techniques to be used in the training initiatives. These decisions can directly affect whether training goals are successfully achieved. Although no single training method is by nature superior to any other, the goals of a particular training and development effort may be better served by one method than another, or one combination of methods versus another combination. The most commonly used training methods will be discussed in the following sections, beginning with on-the-job training.

On-the-Job Training

On-the-job training (OJT) is hardly a new idea. In fact, it has been around so long that it has become a catch-all term for everything an employee learns outside a formal classroom or group training environment. Approximately 90 percent of all industrial training is conducted on the job (Barron, Berger, & Black 1997; Phipps 1996).

More often than not, OJT takes the form of one-on-one instruction: the supervisor or an experienced employee works directly with the trainee, explaining and demonstrating the job, allowing the trainee to practice, and checking and correcting the trainee's work. The experienced employee's major role is that of watching over the individual to provide guidance during practice or learning. For example, sales employees use coaching calls, where a senior sales employee coaches a new sales employees (Bernardin & Russell 1998). Five steps are utilized:

1. Observation of the new employee
2. Feedback obtained by the new employees
3. Consensus (i.e., the coach and the new employee arrived at an agreement as to the positives and negatives for the sales call)
4. Rehearsal of a new sales call
5. Review of the employee's performance (Monoky 1996)

Though OJT is often associated with the development of new employees, it can also be used to update or broaden the skills of existing employees when new procedures or work methods are introduced (Cannell 1997). In its new plant in Alabama, Mercedes-Benz utilizes training circles as a visual record to reveal who is learning what jobs and how quickly their learning is progressing. These are detailed drawings and descriptions of the steps necessary to execute tasks at each workstation. Pie-sized charts are used to indicate the progress of each team member in learning the steps for each task and at what proficiency (Stamps 1997).

OJT is best used when one-on-one training is necessary, only a small number (usually fewer than five) employees need to be trained, classroom instruction is not appropriate, work in progress cannot be interrupted, a certain level of proficiency on a task is needed for certification, and equipment or safety restrictions make other training techniques inappropriate. The training should emphasize equipment or instruments that are to be used, as well as safety issues or dangerous processes (Mullaney & Trask 1992; Filipczak 1996).

Many forms of OJT training focus on exposure to developmental experiences. Job enrichment, job rotation, and apprenticeships are such forms. Job enrichment gradually builds new duties or more challenging responsibilities into an employee's current position, allowing the person to acquire new skills while on the job. Job rotation allows employees to gain experience at different kinds of narrowly defined jobs in the organization. It is often used to give future managers a broad background. Japanese companies are among the best in the world for providing job rotation. Once employees join a firm, the Japanese company spends and enormous amount of money and time training them and exposing them to various job functions. The training is "just-in-time" so that employees are taught skills and then apply their learning within a short period (Overman 1995; Mondy & Noe 1990).

Many companies in the United States have begun to show greater interest in having their employees be able to perform several job functions so that their workforce is more flexible and interchangeable. General Electric requires all managerial trainees to participate in an extensive job rotation program, in which the trainees must perform all jobs they will eventually supervise. This helps managers develop a broader background required for future managerial positions (Bernardin & Russell 1998).

OJT programs are typically associated with the skilled trades derived from the medieval practice of having the young learn a trade from an experienced worker. Apprenticeship programs are often considered OJT programs because they involve a substantial amount of OJT, even though they do consist of some off-the-job training. Typically, the trainee follows a prescribed order of coursework and hands-on experience. The Department of Labor regulates apprenticeship programs, and many require a minimum of 144 hours of classroom instruction each year, as well as OJT with a skilled employee (Reynolds 1993; Gitter 1994). Many professions or trades (e.g., nursing) require some type of apprenticeship program, which may last anywhere from two to five years, although typically the length is five years.

In Europe, apprenticeships are still one of the major ways for young men and women to gain entry to skilled jobs. In the United States, apprenticeships are largely confined to adults looking to work in certain occupations, such as carpentry and plumbing. These apprenticeships generally last four years, and the apprentice's pay starts at about half that of the more experienced "journey workers." Currently only twenty-seven states have apprenticeship agencies and only 2 percent of U.S. high school graduates enter apprenticeships for skilled jobs. One of the consequences of this lack of youth apprenticeship programs is the rapidly shrinking pool of skilled labor in the United States (McKenna 1992).

OJT has both benefits and drawbacks. This type of training is obviously relevant to the job because the tasks confronted and learned are generated by the job itself. Very little that is learned in the context of OJT would not transfer directly to the job. OJT also spares the organization the expense of not only taking employees out of the work environment for training, but also the cost of hiring outside trainers, since company employees generally are capable of doing the training. On the negative side, OJT can prove quite costly to the organization when on-the-job trainees cause customer frustration. Even if only a handful of customers switch to a competitor because of dissatisfaction with service provided by trainees, the cost to the organization can be substantial. Errors and damage to equipment that occur when a trainee is on the job may also prove costly. Another potential drawback is that trainers might be top-notch in terms of their skills but inadequate at transferring their knowledge to others. In other words, those who can, cannot always teach.

Another disadvantage of OJT is when the trainer is like the swimming instructor who thinks that the best way to teach people to swim is to throw them into water over their heads. This method is often only effective by accident. Too often the result is a trainee who has learned some of what is needed to be effective or who blindly followed a demonstration without understanding. The result is that he or she does not do the right thing when left alone on the job. "Sink-or-swim" OJT can produce employees who feel they do not have the right education, question their own intelligence and abilities, and who have little respect or actual resentment for the person who "trained them."

OJT training can save money, since it requires no special training equipment and makes a new hire at least partly productive right away. For mentoring, coaching, and buddy systems, however, these savings must be weighed against the lost productivity of the skilled person assigned to the trainee. For job enrichment and job rotation, the company must anticipate lowered productivity in whatever position the trainee holds. Quality of training can suffer unless a company trains the right employees and managers to serve as coaches and mentors, and selects the right experiences and skills to include in a job rotation or enrichment program.

Properly used, OJT can be one of the most effective forms of training. That is why it continues to be one of the most widely used training methods in many organizations.

Programmed or Self-Instruction

Self-instruction lets trainees learn at their own pace. Topics can range from the simple (vocabulary building) to the complex (strategic planning). Programmed instruction (PI) can be carried out by the use of computers or booklets, depending on the need. The method is to present a small amount of information, followed by a simple question that requires an answer on the part of the learner. There is immediate feedback for each response as the learner finds the answer on the next page or elsewhere. The learner knows whether he or she is right or wrong immediately. Since the program is designed to have a low error rate, the learner is motivated further. The main advantage to such an individualized problem is that it is self-pacing. For remedial instructions, enrichment material, or short segments, this method works well.

Relative to other training methods, self-instruction offers high mobility and flexibility. It can take place with or without instructors, in a wide variety of learning environments (e.g., learning centers, workstations, or homes). It can use formats ranging from print texts to instructional tapes to computers and interactive videodiscs. This flexibility minimizes the disruption to work schedules that training programs can often create. While trainers take a back seat to learners in self-instruction, such programs should have someone monitoring and tracking a participant's progress.

PI is a useful method for self-instruction when the development cost of the materials has been paid by another organization and the materials are available. It might also be a useful method if there are enough trainees to amortize the development cost, and if the material is presented is suitable to the method.

With traditional training unable to keep pace with demand, computers have been used to fill the gap. Computer-assisted instruction (CAI) has become the fastest growing segment of the training industry. Although the costs of CAI are high, compared to costs for formulating and delivering teacher-led courses over a period of several years, the results favor CAI.

Knowledge-based or expert computer systems based on artificial intelligence contain information on particular subjects and can give user-specific advice. Combined with interactive video, expert systems can be used as "intelligent" tutors to teach tasks and skills. The systems can also be used in training that is moving from the transfer of knowledge to the application of the system to goal-oriented tasks in the actual work environment (Becker & Eveleth 1995).

Advantages of PI and CAI include consistency, paced learning, and measurable objectives, among others. Both PI and CAI can reduce total training time appreciably and have the major advantage of immediate feedback. The major drawback is the cost of developing materials.

Computer-Based Training

The rise of computers at work has not only increased the need for computer skills training, but also created new training formats. Computer-based training (CBT) is interactive, self-paced instruction using software teaching tools.

CBT can take a variety of forms. Some employers have formed software libraries containing copies of different tutorial programs that trainees can check out to work on at home. Other companies have staffed computer labs where employees can drop by to practice, with personal assistance available if needed. Still other organizations conduct on-line training, installing learning software on workstation computers that allow employees to switch back and forth between job applications and training programs as their workload demands.

Some companies are attempting to improve the links between training and job applications with computer-based performance support systems, a form of interactive learning. This computer-based tool, also called an electronic support system, a performance support tool, or a knowledge support system, helps employees on the job at the time they need specific information. Although individual programs vary by job, all systems contain a database and a help system.

Performance support systems are useful because participants in a training program can retain only a limited amount of information and usually not as much as has been taught. With a performance support system, however, employees can get training help and information at the exact time needed—the "trainable moment."

Computer-related "knowledge" jobs—such as bank teller positions—in which employees follow certain specified procedures lend themselves most readily to performance support systems. But these systems also help train employees on job tasks that require problem-solving and decision-making skills, such as performance appraisals. Although the costs of developing or purchasing a performance support system can be very high, this expense often is offset by savings realized through improved training delivered in a shorter time.

Use of computers to train employees has become increasingly more common among organizations, especially for training technical skills. As of 1997, it was estimated that 40 percent of U.S. organizations with more than one hundred employees indicated they used CBT (Gordon & Hequet 1997). One leading provider of CBT software, CBT Group, has deals with Cisco Systems, IBM, Informix, Microsoft, Netscape Communications, Novell, Oracle, PeopleSoft, SAP, and Sybase, among others (Informationweek 1997). Training experts believe that by the year 2000, CBT will be the predominant education method for insurance industry employees. For example, Massachusetts Mutual Life Insurance Company uses CBT to train employees and agents (Allen 1996).

Despite the relatively high cost of CBT, it has the advantage of being self-paced, standardized, self-sufficient, easily available, and flexible. This is particularly important in today's fast-paced environment, where organizations cannot afford for employees to be away from the job for large amounts of time. In fact, many training and development personnel see CBT as the most innovative training method ever created. Others view it as a proven way to save time and money while delivering consistent content. For example, CONDUIT (Cooperative Network for Dual-Use Information Technologies) developed new and efficient training techniques based on advanced computer technologies such as simulation, multimedia, and the Internet. The training was for new manufacturing employees and experienced workers who needed to expand their skills. The firm was able to provide more accessible training at a lower cost at local schools and on company PCs (Wiley 1997; Aronson 1996). Clearly, CBT is no longer the "wave of the future," but an available reality, if not necessity.

While annual hardware and software advances make CBT ever more interactive and flexible, a course still takes considerable time and money to develop. However, the cost of developing or purchasing appropriate hardware and software may be offset in other ways. Employers often find these programs are popular among employees, which encourages learning. In addition, some organizations have found that by reducing total training time and minimizing work disruption, CBT pays for its higher implementation costs.

Distance Learning

As many organizations hone their in-house training and development efforts, they are increasingly receptive to so-called "distance learning." What distance learning really does is bring learning closer, often as close as your computer screen. "When you live in a high-tech world that is fast and volatile, you have to be able to deliver knowledge and learning anytime anywhere," says Susan Burnett, manager of business and leadership development at Hewlett-Packard in Palo Alto, California (Greco 1997). The other thing is that organizations have continued to wrestle with the realization that face-to-face education is time out of doing work. And when one factors in traveling time and consumption costs such as hotels and meals when large groups get together, the cost of traditional training and development delivery rises even higher.

With distance learning, a single trainer at one or a number of broadcast sites can deliver a single program, either in real time or synchronously, to multiple learning sites around the world. While it is not clear at this time whether distance learning will ever be a full substitute for traditional live classroom training, it is very likely that at least modularized components will be delivered electronically more and more often as technology improves.

While there are those that believe distance learning will completely replace the old-fashioned training classroom style we are all familiar with, the reality is that people are always going to value one-on-one interaction: reaching out and shaking hands, and gauging body language. That extrasensory element is very important for training professionals as well. They often need that feedback to judge and direct the way a course is proceeding.

Given the current state of technology, it is questionable whether this method is viable for all types of training and development. Casual evidence suggests that distance learning works better with more technical course material (e.g., accounting or statistics) that can be presented via lecture or discussion, and less well with "softer" course material (e.g., team building and strategic thinking) that lends itself to more interactive learning between the trainer and the participants and among the participants themselves. Furthermore, it appears that distance learning is more effective and better received at the lower and middle levels of employees, especially when the focus is on hard, technical skills training.

However, given the potential cost reduction, greater efficiency, and convenience of distance learning efforts, it is a good bet that many organizations will gravitate toward this method and will continue to explore ways of making it more effective. In the short term, experimentation with different formats and applications will continue. In the long run, technological breakthroughs will likely give impetus to dramatic change.

Internet

The Internet offers ways to increase learning, link resources, and share valuable knowledge within and outside an organization. People can use the Internet to deliver training in the following ways, either individually or in combination with other instruction methods:

- E-mail for accessing course material and sharing information
- Bulletin boards, forums, and news groups for posting comments and questions
- Interactive tutorials that let trainees take courses on-line

- Real-time conferencing placing all participants in the same virtual classroom
- Downloading documents, tutorials, and software

The emergence of inexpensive Internet technologies has enabled training professionals to effectively conduct training and provide support to their trainees via the Internet. The advantages of Internet-based training (IBT) are universal language, easy and affordable distribution, fresh content, and cheap technology. Five basic levels of IBT have been developed (Kruse 1997). The first level involves the facilitation of communication between trainers and trainees, while the second is described by the creation of a complete online library of hyperlinked references. The third level involves the automation of the administration of tests and surveys, and the fourth is about the distribution of computer-based training. The fifth level offers delivery of interactive multimedia in real time across an organizational network.

Many of the benefits of IBT are a result of interactivity, or the user's ability to respond to or interact with the software. For example, reading text on the computer is not interactive because the reader passively absorbs information. Computer games, on the other hand, are highly interactive, because the user decides how events will unfold.

The more engaging and interactive the training, the more effective the learning. With IBT, some applications such as hypertext documentation are passive and should be considered support tools. Only when an IBT application is interactive will companies reduce learning time and increase retention through their Internet-based training.

Intranet

In simple terms, the Intranet is the descriptive term being used for the implementation of Internet technologies within a corporate organization, rather than for external connection to the global Internet (Gery 1996). The primary advantage of an Intranet lies in the ability to focus the content to a particular purpose while conquering many of the technology limitations inherent in the World Wide Web (www). Intranet developers are able to limit the identity of users, controlling the access to sensitive information. They also can control bandwidth reservation, assuring quality connection between client and server (Sonntag 1997).

For training professionals, a continual challenge is to keep courseware and training materials up to date regardless of changes to company products or strategic direction. A website on the Intranet is an effective tool to tackle this problem. Those responsible for training and development in their organizations have an obligation to make information readily and meaningfully accessible. With the Intranet, trainers can provide employees access to current training materials incorporating text, graphics, video and audio, available in a self-directed mode at the PC and accessible regardless of geographic location. Through the Intranet training, professionals can permit a high degree of interactivity, enabling topical discussion on bulletin boards, testing, and research. For example, a new field sales hire in Germany may want to simply review the "Value-Added Selling" portion of the new hire orientation training. At the click of a hypertext link and at his or her convenience, the new hire finds the information without having to rummage through reams of desktop manuals.

Some Intranets can also support the delivery of CD-ROM-based training. As CD-ROM programs continue to become more sophisticated, trainers can learn more about them through the use of "authoring" software, which ranges in difficulty from straightforward, template-based programs to more complex applications requiring expert programming skills.

For many companies, training (and other human resources functions) has turned out to be one of the major users of the Intranet. Computer manufacturer Hewlett-Packard recently completed an on-line, world-wide conference for about 2,000 employees involved in education and training (Greco 1997). Since Hewlett-Packard is so decentralized that departments must pay for such education, normal conference attendance would have been much lower. Training its trainers on-line saved the company and its far-flung business units and departments the expense of flying people around the world for a traditional two- or three-day conference. In addition to cost savings for both presenter and attendees, "asynchronous computer conferencing" offers a superb advantage, in that it allows attendees to pop in and out of the virtual goings-on at their convenience.

One advantage to using the Intranet is that employees do not have to work around a set schedule, and they will have a complete written record of what transpired. Negative aspects include the fact that not every organization is equipped with super-fast lines, and also that for many people simply typing and reading can lack the impact more typical of, say, satellite downlinks.

Experts warn that although technologies like the Intranet may provide cost savings, these technologies should not be thought of as cheap alternatives (Greco 1997). In many instances, the mistake made with Intranets is that programming is not designed to maximize benefits. For example, there needs to be a lot less reading going, and information has to be broken down into chunks. Designers who use such technologies should also make sure that the sites used include lots of graphics and offer a good use of the screen in terms of navigation.

Simulations

Particularly effective in training are simulations. Simulations are training tools that attempt to replicate the actual job duties and/or working environment. They vary from simple and inexpensive to highly complex and costly. Organizations often use simulations when the information to be mastered is complex, the equipment used on the job is expensive, and/or the cost of a wrong decision is quite high.

The airline industry has long used simulators to train pilots. Flight simulations often include motion in addition to visual and auditory realism. This aspect substantially increases the cost of the simulation but makes the training even more realistic. Another type of simulation confronts trainee doctors with an accident victim arriving at the emergency. The trainees choose from a menu of options, with the patient dying if the decision is delayed too long or is incorrect.

Traditionally, simulators have been considered separate from CBT with recent advances in multimedia technology; however, the distinctions between these two methods have blurred considerably. In fact, as the technology develops, simulators are becoming more affordable, and hence accessible, for a wider range of organizations.

In-baskets, one of the least expensive simulations, consist of nothing more than the incoming materials, all demanding action, that might get deposited daily on a manager's or secretary's desk. Vestibule training, on the other hand, involves setting up a classroom that reproduces the equipment and work environment, whether an assembly line, switchboard, or city block, found on the job. For certain positions, such as nuclear power plant operators or airline pilots, where the consequences of mistakes could destroy costly machinery or endanger lives, trainees use "simulators" that imitate the functions performed by actual equipment.

With the exception of OJT, simulations are the most realistic and relevant training technique. Unlike on-the-job training, however, simulations allow trainees time to practice skills, receive feedback, and engage in trial-and-error learning—without the embarrassment, cost, time pressures, or other negative consequences of making mistakes while performing a job.

Virtual Reality

Virtual reality (VR) uses a number of technologies to replicate the entire real-life working environment rather than just several aspects of it, as in simulations. Within these three-dimensional environments, a user can interact with and manipulate objects in real time.

Motorola is an example of a company adapting VR for training purposes. Through its Motorola University, the company is testing PC-based VR technology by reproducing an assembly-line setting in which employees will be trained. Traditionally, employees were sent to one of three training centers around the world for a three-day, hands-on training class. The cost of transporting and lodging trainees was high, and the demand for training outstripped the availability. Motorola had previously attempted to set up additional sites that physically recreated the assembly line, but found that installing them was difficult and that getting the necessary machiners was expensive (Minehan 1996). In July 1994, Motorola began to explore VR technology as a solution. Programmers created a computer model replicating an assembly line and its activities. Through VR, the sights and sounds of the assembly line were recreated to make sure the student would feel confident after returning to the actual plant. Preliminary tests produced favorable results. Employees who trained through VR technology scored consistently higher on tests of skills than those who trained by traditional methods. Trainers reported that employees using head-mounted displays spent more time practicing their tasks and appeared to be more enthusiastic and absorbed. Motorola plans to expand its training to a larger pool of students and compare the results with its first experiment.

Tasks that are good candidates for VR training are those that require rehearsal and practice, working from a remote location, or visualizing objects and processes that are not usually accessible. VR training is also excellent for tasks in which there is a high potential for damage to equipment or danger to individuals. One such task is marshaling, an Air Force operational job in which a person on the ground uses hand and arm signals to help a plane land. Imagine the stress one would feel the first time he or she rehearsed these maneuvers with a multiton aircraft approaching at high speed. It is easy to see why VR training is used to prepare people to handle the real situation (Middleton 1992).

Early studies have indicated a great deal of success with VR training. The immersion of trainees in a virtual world may be the key to this success. The VR experience provides a sense of self-location in a simulated environment in which objects appear solid and can be navigated around, touched, and lifted. This sense of immersion is probably connected to the excitement and motivation often reported by VR trainees. For example, following VR training of space shuttle flight control and engineering personnel at NASA, trainees commented on how much fun the training was and how it was the "neatest" training experience they'd had (Psotka 1995). Such trainee experiences can only add to the effectiveness of VR training.

One drawback of VR training is that the technology is meant for one individual user at a time rather than multiple participants. Thus, VR training has not been applicable to team training situations. This limitation may soon be overcome, however. The U.S. military is currently developing a VR training system that allows for the cooperative efforts of multiple trainees (Mastaglio & Callahan 1995). The system includes over fifty different human–computer interfaces and can use one of three simulated terrains, with each terrain representing over 15,000 square kilometers of virtual space. The training exercises are based on scenarios used with combat units in field training. While the system is still being refined, it may represent the next wave of virtual training. The prevalence of teams in the workplace demands effective techniques for improving cooperation among people and work groups. VR training may soon be able to meet this need (Gomez-Mejia, Balkin, & Cardy 1998).

Games and Exercises

Games and exercises are one of the most creative and enjoyable training methods. Most training games and exercises have competition (either individual or group), "playing rules," and a designated finish time or final score. These games simulate competition engaged in by departments or other organizations. At least two teams, each of which represent an organization, make decisions concerning their company's operation. Decisions can be made about production, marketing, finance, human resource utilization, and other challenges. Decisions are based on a set of specified economic theories, presented as a model of the economy.

Some simple management games are not based on analyzing complex problems. Instead, emphasis is placed on making good judgments in a minimum amount of time, based on specific problems and limited rules. In simple games, effective strategies can be reached without making too many decisions and without having to use large amounts of managerial know-how. These management games may oversimplify business relationships and give the impression that running a company can be easy, when in fact even the simplest management decisions require the consideration of many factors. When the model is fairly simple, a referee can be responsible for calculating outcomes.

When the model is complex, a computer may be used. The game can be continuous. Teams receive all or part of the results of their decisions on which they make new decisions, thus continuing the game.

As learning activities, games offer a number of advantages. They add variety and zest to training programs, and get learners actively involved. They allow trainees to acquire knowledge, practice and apply skills, review materials, and ultimately achieve course objectives. They are versatile and easily incorporated into different types of training, whether an instructor-led classroom course or a computer-based instructional program.

While games can enhance training by making learning fun, they will only waste time unless trainers relate these exercises to course objectives. After the game has ended, a trainer should review what happened during the game, have participants say what they learned, and ask trainees how they can apply this learning to their jobs.

Case Studies

Case studies use factual, real-life events to illustrate organizational problems and issues. Case studies can be presented through lecture, film, or video, but most case studies are written and handed out as course materials. Participants read the case study and use what they have learned in the program to analyze the situation.

A case study can involve guided analysis, with formal questions prepared by the instructor for individuals or groups to answer. More challenging case studies use a less structured format and exercise two types of problem-solving skills. Diagnostic analyses ask trainees to identify the underlying cause of a particular problem. Prescriptive analyses require learners to figure out solutions to a particular problem.

Case studies tie course concepts and skills into practical situations. This link, along with the chance to exchange ideas and practice problem solving, enhances trainees' interest and involvement in the program. Trainers can use this technique for either individual or small-group instruction. However, case studies often are complicated and work best when trainees have good analytical reasoning abilities. When presented in a written format, case studies also require that trainees possess well-developed verbal communication and reading comprehension skills.

Classroom Instruction

Classroom lectures are used in many organizations to impart information to trainees. Classroom lectures are oral presentations covering particular topics and concepts. Lectures can last an entire class period and are ideal for presenting large amounts of information to groups. Lecturettes are short lectures lasting less than fifteen minutes. They provide participants with the theoretical background needed for learning new skills. Lecturettes can be combined with question-and-answer sessions, discussions, or other instructional methods.

Discussions involve more interchange and less structure than other oral instructional methods. Discussions encourage participants and trainers to freely exchange knowledge, ideas, and opinions on a particular subject. Discussions work well when the information presented can be applied in different ways. Discussions also give trainers feedback on how employees are using the knowledge or skills they have learned.

Though widely viewed as "boring," classroom instruction can be exciting if other presentation techniques are integrated with the lecture. For example, a videotape could complement the discussion by providing realistic examples of the lecture material.

Demonstrations, Behavior Modeling, and Role Plays

Demonstrations are visual instructional techniques: The instructor performs the behavior or skills to be learned, and the trainees learn by watching. Modeling takes demonstrations one step further by having trainees learn by doing, not just by watching. First, the trainer demonstrates the desired performance, and then participants model the skill or behavior. The trainer provides feedback to trainees, with additional modeling and practice as needed.

Role plays are the most sophisticated of these three instructional methods. After the trainer models the desired skills or behaviors, trainees are asked not just to imitate the trainer's performance, but also to apply these skills and behaviors to a sample situation in which different individuals play certain roles. Solving and discussing problems helps trainees learn technical material and content, and role plays are an excellent way of applying the interpersonal skills being emphasized in the training. If done well, role plays give trainees the opportunity to integrate new information with job behavior (Estabrooke & Fay 1992).

All three techniques can be used in either one-on-one or group instruction. Each method can enhance training by illustrating how to apply instruction in practice. Demonstrations are ideal for basic skills training, while role playing works well for building complex behaviors such as interpersonal or management skills. Of the three tools, demonstrations are the least threatening to trainees, since they are not called on to perform themselves. Modeling and role plays, on the other hand, allow trainers to assess participants' skill levels and to make sure that trainees can apply what they have seen.

SELECTING AND COMBINING METHODS

To choose the training method or combination of methods that best fits a given situation, trainers should first define carefully what they wish to teach. That is the purpose of the needs analysis phase discussed in Chapter 2. Only then can trainers choose a method that best fits these requirements. To be useful, the method should meet the minimal conditions needed for effective learning to take place; that is, the training method(s) should: motivate the trainee to improve his or her performance; clearly illustrate desired KSAOCs; allow the trainee to participate actively; provide an opportunity for practice; provide timely feedback on the trainee's performance; provide some means for reinforcement while the trainee learns; be structured from simple to complex tasks; be adaptable to specific problems; and encourage positive transfer from the training to the job.

As evidenced from the previous section of this chapter, trainers have a wide variety of methods, materials, and media from which to choose when designing and delivering training. Which training techniques best suit a particular program depends on course content and cost considerations. Most training initiatives can use multiple instructional methods and training aids.

Each of these methods described has certain strengths and weaknesses. As a result of the strengths and weaknesses of the various methods, those responsible for training can handle the trade-offs in at least two ways. They can perform a systematic trade-off analysis and choose the most appropriate training methodology. They can also combine training methods. It is apparent from the discussion of the training methods earlier that with a careful analysis, trainers should be able to combine different methods and come up with a more complete and efficient training system. This is in fact what many of those responsible for training are currently doing. In many cases, trainers will use several different techniques (Digman 1980). For example, teaching supervisors how to give performance feedback may first begin with a lecture or overview of the performance appraisal process, followed by small-group discussions or videotapes depicting effective coaching, and then role plays to have supervisors practice their feedback skills (Bernardin & Russell 1998).

The decision of which training methods to use takes on a new dimension when framed by experiential learning theory. For training professionals, the question of which training methods are best can be better answered when learning, the learning process, and individual learning styles are examined, as discussed in Chapter 3. Kolb's model of experiential learning provides a good theoretical basis for understanding this process and for developing and managing decisions on training methods (especially those that are experientially oriented). Clearly, cases, games, and simulations offer learners a rich and more robust view of the workplace environment than, for example, the traditional lecture, or programmed or computer-related methods. But it is also clear that even these methods have a place in the learning cycle. Today more than ever, those responsible for training must be willing to experiment with new technologies and new experiential training methods in an effort to prepare their learners for an ever-changing workplace. Still, if our Internet, case, and simulation methods speak only to the analytic learner, all other learners will not benefit; but, if the training methods created move learners around the learning cycle, then all the participants will find value in the training.

It is clear that there is still much to learn about the effectiveness of training methods like cases, games, simulations and experientially oriented training methods. Whether those responsible for training use one or a combination of training methods, a basic understanding of the learning process may be as important as an understanding of the needs analysis that drives training.

When designing training in the future, training professionals must work under a new "learning paradigm," where the design of learning initiatives is learner centered and controlled, and essentially experiential, while continuing to replace the old "training paradigm" where learning is trainer and content centered. Training professionals must make the important changes in thinking and behavior affecting the design of training and the methods they use to enhance learning, the roles both they and learners fulfill, and their expectations regarding learning outcomes. In conclusion, training professionals must realize the importance of emphasizing a "designing to learn" focus in all their future training and development efforts.

CONCLUSION

The development of the Internet and relatively new focus on the Intranet leave those responsible for training with possibilities limited only by the extent to which they are willing to use their imaginations. Since the National Science Foundation gave up control of the Information Superhighway in late 1994, permitting commercial applications on the Internet for the first time, technology development can only be described as exponential.

It is clear that the World Wide Web (www) and Intranet can be used as an education and training aide, providing available information in moments. And, because it is free of many of the bandwith problems slowing aspects of www–Internet development, some useful training applications will be available on the Intranet before they are generally ready on the Web.

Along with the latest and newest training methods, training professionals have a wide variety of methods they can use to help employees acquire new KSAOCs. Technology will continue to have a major impact on the delivery of training efforts. Further advances in personal computers will continue to permit the use of multimedia training presentations in which sound, animation, photographs, and video will be integrated into the exciting delivery of training initiatives. However, having state-of-the art instructional technology should not be the guiding force in choosing a training method. The specific training method(s) used should be based on the training and development objectives.

CHAPTER 5

Leadership Development

Many organizations have undergone wrenching transformations during the 1980s and 1990s in order to compete effectively on a global scale. With customer value, sustainable revenue growth, and shareholder value, the key criteria for business success, organizations have been seeking to lower costs and increase efficiency by downsizing, delayering, improving processes, and outsourcing.

Today, management training and development has become an important element as organizations attempt to gain a competitive advantage (Kotter 1996). Data suggest that in 1996, an estimated $45 billion was spent on training, and $12 billion was spent on executive education and developing leaders (Ivancevich 1998). *Training's 1997 Industry Report* (Training 1997) estimates that U.S. companies spent $14.5 billion, roughly 25 percent of their training budgets on managers in 1997. Money is not the only commitment either; executives like Roger Enrico of Pepsico and Larry Bossidy of Allied Signal are spending significant amounts of their business days personally teaching future leaders within their organization. It is becoming increasing clear that developing management and executive talent is not a luxury, but a necessity in order to compete (American Productivity & Quality Center 1998). Clearly, organizations have been willing to make the investment in management development in recent years.

This chapter discusses management (later to be referred to as leadership) development and its changing role in organizations. After discussing recent changes in management development in organizations the chapter will offer a brief discussion of the role of management development in organizations. Next, different approaches to management development will be discussed along with criteria for determining which approaches or combination of approaches can best maximize management development efforts. Finally, the chapter will discuss individual leadership development plans (ILDPs) as a tried and tested tool for improving leadership development initiatives.

THE CHANGING FACE OF MANAGEMENT (LEADERSHIP) DEVELOPMENT

As organizations continue to grapple with the threats and opportunities of continuous change, reports of restructuring and refocusing are common, as are daily accounts of mergers, acquisitions, joint ventures, and other strategic alliances. All of these changes have clearly impacted management development. As with organizations, the management development functions who have simply tried to do more of the same now find themselves in serious trouble. Not only is there increased pressure to contribute to achieving important organizational results, but with the urgent need for organizations to be more globally competitive, management development has taken on major importance and undergone a shift in emphasis. Historically, organizations viewed management development purely as a means of bringing managers up to speed on fundamental skills, such as the basics of marketing and finance and techniques for supervising employees.

Management development efforts are also being used to spur organizational change. For instance, a management development effort might be designed to transform a traditional organizational culture into one that emphasizes continuous improvement, organizational learning, and total quality management. Clearly, management development is an important element in organizational efforts to improve their competitiveness and achieve their strategic agendas.

The new paradigm of management development focuses on enhancing an organization's effectiveness while simultaneously maintaining a competitive advantage (Ulrich & Lake 1990; Burack, Hochwarter, & Mathys 1997). It is increasingly global in outlook (Baird et al. 1994) and builds on a "seamless" organizational structure that minimizes functional, unit, and international border lines (Ulrich 1992). It is building organizational excellence through the continuous alignment of organizational members, business process, and structures with vision, values, strategies, and learning (Robinson & Wick 1992). Sir Paul Girolami, Chairman of Glaxo (U.K.) described critical features of this newer perspective and approach as follows: "Emphasis is on leadership and quality of management, rather than central authority and command: trust and partnership rather than bureaucratic control." Thus, this orientation defines the corporate "centre" (headquarters) as one that specifies global strategies, and exerts functional control, establishes standards, and provides orientation (Osbaldeston & Barham 1992, 18). Programs are increasingly customized and systematical relative to individual needs (Burack, Hochwarter, & Mathys 1997).

Underlying the new paradigm in management development is the assimilation of management development efforts with strategic planning along with efforts to teach the more intangible aspects of leadership, market–client thinking (which is often cross-cultural), adaptability, implementation strategies, and change management (Gupta 1992; Vicere 1992). Strategically linked management development activities that include specific assignments along with education and training are intended to go a long way toward accomplishing these kinds of learning. The goal is to obtain the fullest use of human resource capabilities by developing managers to assume positions of greater responsibility.

Recent consulting and research experience show remarkable convergence in newer management development thought whether dealing with American, European, or Pacific Rim firms (Osbaldeston & Barham 1992; Howes & Foley 1993). In each of these domains, the prevalent theme involves the integration of management development activities with strategic goals to attain a competitive advantage (Cappelli & Hefter-Crocker 1996). Recurring management development objectives for performance improvement and effectiveness include: management of organizational change and adaptation to unique situations; reducing cycle time for virtually every major process and activity; promoting continuous learning and improvement; introducing and extending quality management principles and practices; managing cultural diversity and also cross cultural communications; and building leadership and relational skills (Burack, Hochwarter, & Mathys 1997).

Human knowledge and competencies have strategic importance in that they are the counterpart to the core competencies of their corporation. This recognition then becomes a logical point-of-entry to the effective learning organization. Management development plays a key role in its accomplishment (Baird et al. 1994; Robinson & Wick 1992). In addition, long-term competitiveness depends on fully developing and using all of the expertise and talent in the organization. Also, knowledge-based organizations have "know-how" as their main asset, and continuous development is becoming a way of organizational life (Ulrich 1992).

High-performing, leading organizations are increasingly distinguished by a number of the features of their management development approaches. Their sustained profitability and general management effectiveness provide benchmarks for virtually all organizations regardless of size and geographic scope of operations (Burack, Hochwarter, & Mathys 1997). These features are as follows (Burack, Hochwarter, & Mathys 1997; Vicere & Fulmer 1998; Bardach 1997):

1. *Management development clearly linked to business plans and strategies.* General competency development is still a necessary condition but not a sufficient one. The fast pace of change demands a faster cycle time for development, application, and change (Allee 1996). Increasingly, management development designs are initiated by business priorities and imperatives while continuing the individual's progress. The key point is the importance of linking management development to an organization's overall strategic direction (i.e., management development efforts are clearly driven by the extent to which the process flows logically from a company's strategic agenda). The focus of the process is to identify and develop the talents and perspectives that the organization needs to achieve its long-term strategic objectives. Specific initiatives are built around a market-oriented focus, coupled with a strong element of competitive analysis, to help managers at *all* levels understand the strength and weaknesses of the organization and what it will take to build competitive advantage. This understanding is related to the organization itself—the systems, structures, processes, goals, and relationships necessary for success in a highly competitive world.

2. *Management development that emphasizes integrating overall corporate strategy, marketing, and technology.* Historically, the emphasis in management development in organizations has been on the management of technology—that is, on teaching managers how best to manage the research and development function in order to produce technologically driven or enhanced products and services. The new direction of management development aims to provide the KSAOCs that will make it possible for managers to conceptualize and manage at the intersection of strategy, marketing, and technology. The object is not to convert managers into technologists, but rather to provide managers with the insights and understanding they need in order to use technology to create a unique competitive advantage based on customer needs. Some basic elements of successful management development include the following ideas.

3. *Globalization and cross-cultural orientation.* The development activities are internationally focused on successfully meeting challenging communication issues. The vast majority of management development efforts recognize the broad implications of internationalization to all aspects of business life, from working on multifunctional–multiregional product design teams, to the running of transnational firms that have shareholders, employees, customers, suppliers, and creditors all over the world. Even though the firm may be small or domestically oriented in terms of product or service, economic, competitive, and sourcing considerations dictate their global outlook (Dowling & Welch 1991), as they acknowledge that global issues impact all levels and dimensions of the organization. The importance of this reality is highlighted by Bolt's (1989) research which sug-

gests that competition resulting from an increase in internationalization was the factor most likely to affect future management development strategies. Consequently, globalization of management development often means conducting real or virtual classes in different parts of the world, sometimes in more than one language, for a geographically heterogeneous group of participants, with an international faculty whose members have a diverse set of teaching, research, and consulting experiences.

4. *Seamless.* Organizations until recently developed managerial layers as they grew to help the company with coordination, control, reporting, and succession issues. However, more recently, organizations have acknowledged the adverse effects of excessive layers. Shaw and Schneider (1993) suggest that increased politics, faulty and delayed decision making, and ineffective communications occur when organizations get "too tall." Simply reducing layers without leadership training would not necessarily lead to success. Cappelli and Crocker-Hefter (1996) note that management development programs that focus on leadership will only succeed if they instill a sense of confidence in the employee. Deep-seated changes in individual attitudes and mindsets often represent one of the greatest challenges in developing management development efforts. Like any training initiative in an organization, a sincere commitment from top management to fully support new management development initiatives and roles are a part of successful programs.

5. *Management development that provides the organization with "glue" to integrate subsidiaries and other units that need their own autonomy.* The role of management development has changed from a long-standing focus on "getting the right people into the right places at the right times" through recruitment, succession planning, training, and other forms of development (Brewington 1996). The new paradigm of management development has become a tool for organizational development that helps drive flexibility, commitment, and competitiveness of the entire organization (Vicere & Fulmer 1998).

6. *Corporate culture and the particularization of management development designs.* The importance of maintaining a shared set of expectations and values has been discussed with great voracity over the years (Byrne 1969; Chatman 1989; Judge & Ferris 1992; Schein 1990). Trust and commitment are critical elements. The philosophy of management, organizational values, and corporate histories further shape individual learning priorities and preferred practices. These affect management development procedures and desired outcomes. In 1990, Robert Horton of British Petroleum (BP) initiated "Project 1990." The goal of the project was to culturally prepare the organization for the environment of the next century.

7. *Core competencies.* These are both general and technical and, when kept up to date for positional mobility, grow exponentially with use. Failure to apply these core competencies, however, causes them to be extinguished eventually (Prahalad & Hamel 1990). The core competencies of individuals are thoughtfully linked to the core competencies of the organization. High priority business outcomes often dictate the timing and convergence

of these accomplishments. In addition, certain characteristic skills appear increasingly needed whether the organization is situated in Europe, Australia, the Pacific Basin, or America.

8. *A decreased emphasis on management development and an increased focus on leadership.* Vicere and Fulmer (1998) have recently noted that in today's changing business environments, traditional processes for developing leadership talent are in such a state of flux that a new vocabulary is emerging. There is little interest in the old mainstay term *management development*. Managers today are often viewed as bureaucrats whose function is to create complexity and preserve the status quo. *Executive education* is a more desirable term, but in today's flatter, more networked organizations, there is less demand for "executives," often viewed as aloof and removed from the realities of the competitive marketplace. And the word education connotes the esoteric contemplation of academic issues, a process at odds with today's fast-paced business environment. Vicere and Fulmer (1998) point out that there does seem to be great interest in the term *leadership development* (which will be used instead of management development for the remainder of this chapter), which characterizes processes for identifying and developing exceptional people capable of moving an organization into the twenty-first century. People who can broaden the horizons of participants so that they can see and understand different realities or alternative courses of action.

9. *Focus on growing and developing entrepreneurial leaders.* This demand has arisen as an outgrowth of downsizing, decentralization, and cost reduction, along with a renewed emphasis on growing the top line profitably. Small has become beautiful, as long as it is combined with flexibility, responsiveness, and ingenuity to meet customer needs in a profitable way. Given the complexity of business in today's highly competitive international marketplace, significant advantages can be attained by combining small size with the economies of scale, purchasing power, and sophisticated systems of infrastructures in large corporations. Leadership development initiatives are expected to grow to develop people who have the KSAOCs that enable them to successfully think and act like entrepreneurs.

10. *Individual learning focused within the context of organizational learning.* Experiential learning, continuous learning, and adaptation are program hallmarks (Senge 1990a). Approaches thoughtfully combine on-the-job experiences and formal programmed learning in both individual and group situations. Individual, group, and unit learning are coordinated (Mullen & Lyles 1993). To many organizations, setting up a learning environment is a relatively novel idea, while others have been in the process for years. For example, general managers at Motorola were asked to write a paper each year discussing their achievement and indicating what they learned in the process. The systematic repetition of these activities makes organizational learning habitual.

11. *A career development focus.* This is needed to build individual trust and commitment. Central authority and command are deemphasized, and trust and partnership are emphasized. Systematic needs analyses are tailored

to the individual and are oblivious to race and gender issues. Age and maturity factors are viewed in the framework of individual work, career, and life cycles. Recent research found that successful and unsuccessful firms conducted organizational career development (OCD) activities differently. For example, successful companies received commitment from top leaders at the inception of the program, established tangible guidelines, worked in a bottom-up fashion, and remained flexible (Gutteridge, Leibowitz, & Shore 1993, 81).

12. *Benchmarking for program improvement.* Searching out and examining highly effective leadership development practices by experienced benchmarkers to adopt the best and adapt them to their own organizations is an ongoing occurrence. It provides direction and clear targets, and it allows the organization to determine both what is being done (compared to similar organizations and programs) and where progress is needed to improve overall performance. Benchmarking is used to advance performance through careful implementation and continuous refinement of leadership development efforts. Several critical success factors to the benchmarking process are in place. These factors are a well-designed performance measurement and benchmark system; senior leadership support; customer responsiveness; benchmarking training for the leadership development team; and resources, especially in the form of time, funding, and personnel, that enable the benchmarking of leadership development to be effective. Benchmarking is used to ensure that leadership development initiatives set and meet strategic expectations or targets.

13. *Leadership development contributes to the bottom line and no longer relies on its intrinsic value to demonstrate its real worth to the organization.* Increasingly, it has been transformed along with the changes affecting the organization. With this transformation, leadership development is subjected to increased accountability and a requirement to show a measurable contribution to the organization.

14. *A leadership development function that adapts measurement processes and in some cases leadership development functions that turn into profit centers.* In this respect, leadership development is just one of many organizational functions that were traditionally taken for granted as necessary and unmeasurable and were forced to respond to pressures to show their contribution in measurable terms.

The sea change in leadership development features presented above can serve as the basis for benchmarking leadership development in any organization. The changes that have been going on in organizations and their leadership development focus provides a clear view of the future of leadership development that responds to customer needs. This simply means delivering leadership development initiatives that are better, cheaper, and faster. Better means providing insights, KSAOCs, tools, and perspectives that enable leaders to effectively address current and projected organizational needs and challenges.

Cheaper means leadership development experiences provide a higher learning yield for every corporate dollar expended. And faster means quicker design and delivery of leadership development programs, as well as shorter-duration learning experiences, faster response times, and more program evaluations. In other words, it is becoming increasingly apparent that leadership development must have the same fundamental characteristics as most products and services.

THE ROLE OF LEADERSHIP DEVELOPMENT IN THE ORGANIZATION

For leadership development to have its intended organizational and individual impact under the new paradigm the commitment of the organization is absolutely critical. Those responsible for today's and tomorrow's leadership development cannot afford to take the organization's commitment for granted. The real test of the organization's commitment can ultimately only be found in funding, senior leadership participation, attendance, ongoing program evaluation, and the extent to which leadership development is an equal partner in the organization's overall strategic plan.

Like any commitment on behalf of senior leadership there is no one way to ensure their commitment to leadership development. However, one way to determine whether there is commitment to leadership development is in a documented vision or policy that specifically makes clear the role and purpose of leadership development. The existence of such a vision or policy should help establish and give meaning to leadership development in the organization. This means that leadership development exists to support the organization's overall goals or strategic agenda.

In any case, mere organizational statements without true senior executive or top leadership support are meaningless. Senior leadership must be willing to document how specific examples of leadership development will contribute to accomplishing agreed upon goals. It is just as important to have all levels of the organization's leadership accountable for attainment of these objectives, starting with top leadership, which must lead by example. Accountability implies the need to have measurable ways to check on the progress.

Like any other initiative undertaken in the organization, once top leadership is committed to the role of leadership development in achieving organizational results, a thorough needs analysis must be conducted to determine what the specific goals and objectives are for leadership development in support of the organizational vision and expected results. Senior leadership is the best source of information on what needs to be done. However, the broader customer base (current and future leaders and others in the organization) should be consulted for their input. Including others' input in the design of leadership development efforts early on goes a long way toward ensuring ownership of the efforts and a greater stake in the outcome. It is very important for those responsible for leadership development efforts to avoid being the sole owner of leadership development initiatives in the organization. Again, leadership development must be viewed as a key element in the achievement of the organization's visions and achievement of expected results. Brewington (1996) notes that it is the role of leadership development to make this connection as a part of the organization's commitment to its vision and thus to leadership development. This point cannot be overstated, and those responsible for leadership development must always be attentive to ensuring that leadership development is part of the overall organizational strategy and vision.

As highlighted in the discussion on collecting data during the needs analysis in Chapter 2, gaining greater involvement by all in the organization can be as simple as asking them. Those responsible for leadership development efforts should conduct one-on-one interviews, regularly participate in departmental meetings, leadership roundtables, and use a survey to gather information necessary to determine what should be done. Again, as many of these opportunities as are practical should be used to collect pertinent information.

Building customer demand early into the design, delivery, and evaluation of leadership development efforts will ensure that it has an ongoing, customer-driven focus. Customer input should be the *modus operandi* during each cycle of the leadership development process. This point is especially important when determining how to measure the effectiveness of leadership development efforts. Including customers in the decision of which results can reinforce leadership development's support of the overall organizational strategy will go a long way in keeping leadership development a part of the organization's main agenda.

Ultimately, the goal of senior leadership support throughout the leadership development process is to ensure that leaders are provided with effective learning experiences and environments—ones in which they are challenged to resolve both old and new problems using appropriate tools and KSAOCs; where they learn from their experiences and share knowledge and experiences with colleagues; and where they have opportunities to grow intellectually and emotionally as leaders.

There is no question that many organizations emphasize short-term results and tend more and more to impose these expectations on leadership development. While those responsible for leadership development in organizations need to ensure that participants are furnished with the KSAOCs they need to perform better in their current and future jobs, the real payoff of leadership development frequently comes much farther down the road. Successful leadership development initiatives will allow neither themselves nor their organizations to lose sight of this.

One of the most important decisions to make is how to deliver the management development initiatives. The considerations are many and the implications equally numerous. For example, using internal versus external sources to deliver the leadership development initiatives presents a number of decisions that must be made by all stakeholders involved in the process. Fortunately, as noted in the next section, the options on how to deliver the leadership development initiatives are plentiful, and the decision must be made not solely on the basis of getting the job done but as part of the overall organizational plan.

LEADERSHIP DEVELOPMENT APPROACHES

There are numerous approaches and types of leadership development. Leadership development systems usually incorporate more than one of the following approaches in their management development efforts.

Company Schools

Several large companies have their own "universities" for leaders. Two of the most notable of these are Motorola and McDonald's. Company schools educate both current and potential leaders in the corporate culture, leadership philosophy, and KSAOCs, as well as the methods of doing business.

University-Based Programs

These programs can be grouped into several broad categories, with a host of subcategories. Three broad market segments are general leadership programs, shorter open-enrollment programs, and customized programs. Many business schools offer these types of programs designed specifically for leaders. Programs at schools like Harvard, Cornell, Darden, Stanford, and the University of Michigan rely heavily on the case study method, in which students do in-depth analyses of real-life companies. General leadership programs typically address each of the major management disciplines and place them in the contexts of strategic thinking and, increasingly, of change management. Shorter, open-enrollment programs include programs that are two weeks or less in length and focus on one leadership function or theme, or on a highly delimited set of these. Customized, company-specific programs are designed to meet a predetermined set of company-specific needs.

Other Types of Approaches

Whether leadership development is provided in a company, school, university business school, or (as is most often the case) a less formal setting, the effort often utilizes special techniques. One such technique is role-playing, in which participants adopt the role of a particular leader placed in a specific situation—for instance, a leader who has to give a negative performance review to an employee. Leadership games are elaborate role-playing exercises in which multiple participants enact a leadership situation.

Programs focusing on organizational culture and values, human resources, financial management, marketing, labor relations, leadership theory, information systems, government requirements, and the like can help expand leaders' horizons. Many organizations offer such courses as part of their in-company leadership development initiatives. However, many other organizations find it is easier and less expensive to use outside training resources. For instance, recent study results indicate that organizations traditionally tend to outsource the design, development, and delivery of leadership development programs, while keeping much of the needs assessment and program evaluation in-house (Walters 1997).

It is important to understand that when designing developmental experiences, organizational leaders and HRD professionals should set up a system to analyze and review the leadership candidate's progress during the trial period. Leaders at different levels need feedback for the experience to serve as learning rather than a sink-or-swim situation. This technique requires communication among the participant, their immediate boss, peers, direct reports, higher level leaders, and an HRD professional.

Outsourcing of leadership development efforts centers primarily around issues of expertise and cost. The single most important factor in the outsourcing decision is to acquire content expertise in leadership issues. The Walters (1997) study did note, however, that there has been an increasing trend to furnish in-house leadership development programs. An important value of having in-house programs lies in the ability to use employees from other functional areas such as HR, sales, engineering, or finance, and top leadership as facilitators and teachers. Experienced leaders often lend enormous credibility to the practical side of what is being taught or implemented. This practice allows the individual, a content expert through hands-on practice, to share company and industry-related experience. On the other hand, having expertise in other areas does not automatically qualify the individual to be an effective facilitator or teacher. The following discus-

sion highlights different developmental experiences that HRD professionals and their organizations can use to help prepare leadership candidates for promotion.

Classroom Training

Today's leaders need a broad range of KSAOCs. Some areas in which
they may need ongoing training and development include the following: changes in the organization's strategic direction; organization culture and organizational development; competitive external business
environment; interorganizational communication and links; performance and productivity improvement; team building; HRD issues; and
customer and supplier expectations.

Good selection procedures and classroom training can build leadership KSAOCs important to achieving the organization's strategic
agenda. But putting leadership candidates through various on-the-job
trial experiences can substantially reduce an organization's risk of
putting the wrong person in a key leadership position.

Understudying

This method assigns a current or future leader to work with another
leader for a certain time period. If the organization is grooming the person for a specific leadership position, the individual may understudy one
particular leader. For a broader foundation, understudies may rotate
among several leaders. Using either method, the individual sees the day-
to-day leadership duties, while the leader acts as coach and appraiser.

If the leadership coach is reluctant to delegate or finds it hard to
share job duties with the understudy, the leadership candidate will
gain little from the experience. Understudying is most successful when
the senior leader's attitudes and work techniques are harmonious with
the strategic development objectives of the organization.

Task Force and Project Assignments (TFPAs)

TFPAs provide a valuable source of linking developmental opportunities. Although such assignments are often met with a less than enthusiastic response by those chosen to participate, they can be very effective
developmental experiences (Vicere & Fulmer 1998). TFPAs give organizations a chance to expose developing leaders to different types of
leadership situations, thereby enhancing their potential for development. These experiences also benefit developing leaders by helping
them realize that they cannot be experts on everything, that there are
others within an organization with complementary capabilities who
are essential to both personal and organizational success. Such insights
not only promote individual development but also lay the foundation

for internal leadership networks (McCall, Lombardo, & Morrison 1988), so crucial to the transfer of knowledge throughout the organization.

Also, at times a leadership vacancy can occur unexpectedly before anyone has been groomed for the job. One option for handling the situation is to appoint the best available prospect as temporary leader. If the leader does well, the placement becomes permanent; if not, then another individual should be appointed as soon as possible. Depending on the position and the individual's progress, the trial period can last anywhere from six weeks to six months.

TFPAs that occur during a regular leader's vacation or absence, or due to an assignment to a special project also can serve developmental purposes. By stepping into leadership positions even for a brief period, individuals gain practical experience that prepares them for the real thing. As a bonus, senior leadership can see how an individual handles a particular leadership position or situations.

For the experience to prove worthwhile, temporary or acting leaders should have full leadership powers. Some organizations even avoid letting direct reports know that their leader is actually a temporary appointment.

Partial Assignment of Leadership Duties

Some organizations develop their leadership prospects by assigning them a portion of the position's duties and gradually increasing these responsibilities as the individual become proficient. If the individual cannot assume increased responsibilities at the expected rate of progress, the organization may reevaluate its selection.

This method, when combined with understudying, works particularly well in grooming an individual for particular leadership positions. Since the individual assumes the position in phases, he or she is better able to do justice to learning each aspect of the job.

Coaching–Mentoring Programs (CM)

CM programs establish an on-the-job relationship between an experienced leader and a less experienced individual in the same career track. CM is one way high potential employees and less advantaged female and minority employees learn about organizational operations and are groomed for more responsibility. Acting as a CM also can enrich the jobs of plateaued midlevel employees.

Many organizations avoid formal coaching–mentoring programs because successful mentoring often involves "chemistry"—something difficult to assign. Instead, some companies use sponsor programs that have experienced leaders show less experienced individuals the ropes without taking formal responsibility for the leaders' development.

It is also is quite common for organizations to use external mentors–coaches, often consultants or well-known university professors, to provide advice and support senior leaders facing critical issues or challenges. Organizations like the Levinson Institute in Cambridge, Massachusetts, specialize in this activity, as do certain staff at think tanks like the Center for Creative Leadership (Smith 1993; Nai 1994). Traditionally, CM programs generally belong to HRD, although more and more organizations are moving away from assigning oversight to this function.

Action Learning

Although these approaches can create a foundation for the creation and transfer of KSAOCs throughout the organization, action learning can help institutionalize the process. Wick and Leon (1993) noted that action learning helps make experiential learning intentional and deliberate. According to Marsick and his colleagues (1992), action learning involves "learning by doing, but it is not a simulation. . . . It is 'training' that takes the form of an actual business problem for teams of learners to solve together."

Team-based action learning initiatives can be a very powerful mechanism for linking learning both to the workplace and to the strategic agendas of the organization. Through action learning, an organization can convert individual learning into organizational knowledge through the hands-on resolution of real organization problems. Because the projects are conducted in teams, learning is shared across members, networking is reinforced, new perspectives are encouraged, and leadership skills are practiced. All this takes place within the context of the organization's strategic imperatives, helping to bring those imperatives to life and give them meaning throughout the organization. In addition, action learning can help resolve business issues related to the pursuit of strategic imperatives, creating an additional return on investment for the organization.

Compared with other types of training and development, leadership efforts involve few individuals and covers highly specialized subjects. The most commonly used techniques for helping executive development efforts are accomplished through classroom education (internal, external, and consortium), feedback approaches, new learning technologies, coaching–mentoring, and self-improvement–personal growth (Vicere & Fulmer 1996).

In general, outside courses, seminars, and conferences are practical ways for an organization to develop leaders' skills. However, some types of leadership development are better covered through in-house programs. For example, the corporate controller, marketing vice president, or employee relations heads can present overviews of problems facing the organization in the financial, sales, or HR areas. The company's legal counsel likewise can do a better job than an outsider could when explaining how a new law or government regulation affects the organization.

As this discussion demonstrates, there are a variety of leadership development approaches available to organizations. However, decisions must be made on which approaches to use, and the next section offers some criteria for making the necessary decisions.

DECIDING ON DEVELOPMENT APPROACHES

Deciding on a development approach or a combination of approaches must be done by weighing various criteria. The choice can be made on the basis of number of leaders to be developed, relative costs per leader per each method, availability of development materials in various forms (including the instructor's capabilities), and employees' relative efficiency in learning. In general, the more active the leader, the greater the motivation to learn—and thus the higher the probability of success. If there are only a few instructors, individualized programmed instruction may be considered. If none of the leaders are capable of giving certain instructions, outside instructors may be contacted, or movies or videotapes might be used. The method used should reflect the degree of active participation desired for the initiative.

Inevitably, the effectiveness of each form of leadership development must be evaluated. There are studies to support the effectiveness of most methods; if a method is appropriate for the particular initiative in question, it should be used.

The classic debate continues about which development approach or technique is best. Some favor a combination of approaches, while others prefer an array of humanist and behaviorist techniques (Galpin 1996). The techniques of behaviorism include behavioral modeling, role playing, positive reinforcement, and simulations. The preferred techniques of the humanist approach to development (associated with Carl Rogers) include self-assessment, visualization, and guided reflection. There are also advocates of cognitive approaches who believe that lectures, discussion, readings, and debates are the best approach to use (Ivancevich 1998).

The decision on which approach or combination of approaches to use during leadership development initiatives must include some discussion of the complexity of the tasks to be learned. For example, complex tasks such as learning how to be an effective leader of employees often require cognitive and humanistic approaches. Also, the ability of the learner needs to be considered. More sophisticated learners usually require more cognitive approaches and a chance to discuss their viewpoints.

In the end, the leadership development demands of an organization's strategic agenda are best addressed through a balanced portfolio of methods that address both individual and organizational development. Within benchmark companies, there is a clear understanding of the role that each of these methodologies plays in the leadership development process. Work experience is seen as the key driver of individual development. Leadership development initiatives are designed to help build perspective and outline the "why" and "what" of continued individual development. Linking a variety of activities is used to provide hands-on practice, clarifying the "what" and facilitating the "how" of development, ultimately promoting knowledge creation and organizational development. Competency models are created to help the organization institutionalize the "how," as well as define and delineate "who"—who is likely to succeed in a leadership position, how will they perform their duties, and how the organization will assist them to develop to their fullest potential. Together these elements comprise the fundamentals for creating a sound and strategically oriented leadership development process.

SELECTION OF LEADERSHIP DEVELOPMENT CANDIDATES

Historically, at some organizations, career ladders predetermine who will move up to fill a leadership slot that becomes vacant. Selection in this situation occurs early, before the individual moves into the position immediately below the management level.

In most organizations today, however, several equally ranked positions feed into a leadership post, and the company has more formal methods of selecting which of several candidates is best suited to move up. Top leadership, along with HR, may conduct interviews and screening of leadership prospects, with the final decision evolving through group consensus.

Some companies set up formal leadership evaluation teams that assess candidates using established criteria. Along with looking at leadership qualities and leadership styles, the team will evaluate a candidate's suitability in light of the organization's long-range business strategy and succession plans. As discussed in the following section, other organizations send candidates to an assessment center that conducts in-depth evaluations and makes final recommendations. A ten-step individual leadership development plan (ILDP) process to identify candidates for leadership development can also be used by organizations. These ten steps are leadership candidate application and/or nomination; application review; realistic job preview of leadership's job; supervisor appraisal; committee appraisal review; candidate assessment; development of ILDP for future leaders; implementation of ILDP; ongoing follow-up of ILDP assessment; and ongoing interview and reassessment of leader development. A modified version of the ILDP process is discussed later in this chapter.

Leadership Assessment Centers

Assessment centers, which first developed during World War II, have become increasingly popular methods of selecting leadership candidates. Organizations ranging from IBM, AT&T, Ford, Office Depot, Procter & Gamble, Xerox, the Department of Defense, the Federal Aviation Administration, and the CIA have adopted this approach to leadership selection. Assessment centers are expensive; costs range from a low of about $125 for each candidate to as much as $3,000 for upper-level leadership selection.

With the typical assessment center method, information about employee's strengths and weaknesses is provided through a combination of performance tests, which are designed to stimulate the type of work to which the candidate will be exposed. Trained assessors observe and evaluate performance in the situational exercises. The assessors compile and integrate their judgments on each exercise to form a summary rating for each candidate (Bernardin & Russell 1998).

Individual assessment centers operate differently from one another. Assessment center programs tend to vary in purpose and use, such as selection, promotion, training, and development: length of the assessment process (one day to one week); the ratio of assessors to those being assessed; the extent of assessor training; and the number and type of assessment instruments and exercises.

Preevaluation Activities

Prior to the session, the assessment center staff gathers information about the position for which candidates are competing. This process might include reviewing previously conducted job analyses; interviewing incumbents about current job demands; and asking top leadership which aspects of the job are likely to change in the next five to ten years. In addition, assessors find out what qualities have characterized persons who have succeeded and failed in that position and what characteristics are important to future success in the job given the organization's strategic agenda.

Assessment Techniques

Once candidates arrive at the assessment center, they undergo tests and exercises designed to evaluate their leadership potential. Techniques might include the following:

1. *Psychological and aptitude tests.* Candidates typically take a variety of tests to determine whether they possess the knowledge needed by leaders. In addition, assessment centers often administer personality and other aptitude tests that look for leadership skills; decision-making and long-term planning ability; commitment to quality; motivation and career ambitions; written and oral communication skills; independence; tenacity and determination; organization; and ability to handle stress.

2. *In-basket exercises.* Using a sample in-basket, the candidate decides what material requires prompt attention, assigns tasks to direct reports, and dictates responses to letters. Upon completion of the exercise, an assessor may interview candidates to find out what they learned from the exercise and what reasons they used for their decisions.

3. *Group discussions.* In these leaderless activities, candidates either select or are assigned roles in a debate about some issue, such as the type of training needed by college recruits. While a leader is not designated for the group, one usually emerges during the group interaction.

4. *Role plays.* These exercises have candidates act out a specific leadership task, such as interviewing a job candidate or disciplining a subordinate for excessive absenteeism. The subordinate is a trained role player. Another example is to have candidates interact with clients or individuals external to the organization, requiring them to obtain information or alleviate a problem.

5. *Business games.* These group activities assign candidates roles to play in handling different situations that a leader might face.

6. *In-depth interviews.* Assessors usually conduct in-depth interviews covering candidate's childhood experiences, personal goals, reasons for these goals, expectations for the future, and so forth.

7. *Oral presentation.* In the brief time allowed, candidates plan, organize, and prepare a presentation on an assigned topic. An assessment center developed by IBM requires candidates for sales management positions to prepare and deliver a five-minute oral presentation in which they present one of their hypothetical staff members for promotion and then defend the staff member in a group discussion. IBM uses this exercise to evaluate aggressiveness, selling ability, self-confidence, resistance, and interpersonal contact.

8. *Final selection.* After candidates have completed the evaluation activities, the assessors meet to discuss each individual's performance, sharing their notes and spending at least one hour on each candidate. A standardized rating sheet covering about twenty areas is completed for each individual. These sheets allow ready comparison of candidates; the highest rated person typically receives the center's recommendation for the position. Some centers issue final evaluation reports for each candidate, which then can be used by the person's supervisor to plan further training and development activities.

Advantages and Disadvantages of Using Assessment Centers

On the plus side, assessment centers provide one of the most thorough, objective, and well-standardized means of assessing candidates. In addition, research shows good correlations between assessment center ratings and leadership job performance. The primary disadvantage of assessment centers is the cost: Outside assessment centers often charge at least $1,000 per candidate.

In addition to determining the strategic objectives of leadership development initiatives, deciding on a balanced portfolio of approaches to use, and selecting individuals to be developed, organizations must ensure that their efforts are focused on the continuous learning and development of leaders. The final section discusses the individual leadership development plan, which can be a useful tool in the creation and implementation of successful leadership development initiatives.

Individual Leadership Development Plans

Many organizations have implemented the use of employee development plans for all categories of employees. The impetus for the implementation of individual development plans is difficult to pinpoint because they have been used for a variety of purposes. For example, individual development plans have been initiated to support special interest programs, to foster upward mobility for minorities, women, and disabled workers, and to identify employees for other types of positions within an organization. Employee development plans should be viewed as yet another tool to facilitate career development and enhance the quality of development.

Organizations can use individual leadership development plans (ILDPs) to increase both the effectiveness and success of their companies leadership development efforts. ILDPs are driven by an organization's strategic agenda and how it plans to build competitive advantage in the marketplace through its people. The strategic agenda serves as the basis for the establishment of a developmental process for leaders (and other employees) as the organization moves toward the future. The benefits of such an approach appear to be many, including the following:

1. Developing a leader's capabilities is consistent with an organization's HR policy committed to the ongoing development of individuals to reach their highest potential. Leadership development is important in the organizational and career development system.

2. ILDPs enable a leader to acquire the KSAOCs needed for successful performance in the organization. It also eases the transition from an individual's current job to one involving greater career responsibilities.

3. ILDPs assist in leadership recruitment, retention, and morale development. Those organizations that fail to provide such individualized development efforts often lose their most promising leaders. Frustrated with the lack of opportunity, achievement-oriented leaders will often seek employment with other organizations outside that show more commitment to leadership development and provide more incentive with individual growth, development, and learning for career advancement.

4. ILDP efforts can increase an employee's level of commitment to the organization and improve perceptions that the organization is a good place to work. By developing and promoting leaders, organizations create a competent, motivated, and satisfied workforce.

5. ILDPs provide the employer and employee with a systematic long-term plan for leadership development. Improvement areas and learning opportunities are outlined in advance with the employee as they relate to increasing the employee's ability to successfully do leadership work related to the achievement of specific business results. Reducing the guessing game by having the employer outline leadership selection criteria *a priori* is a critical element to the success of this type of development system.

Organizations, their HR functions, and HRD professionals must be prepared to follow a standardized and documented leadership development process, including these several aspects:

- that it be tailored to and based on an analysis of the actual requirements (competence and KSAOCs) of an actual leader's job given expected business results
- that it provide leadership candidates with information about the expectations of the job given the organization's strategic agenda
- that it provide leadership candidates with a developmental assessment of their own competence and KSAOCs (i.e., similar to a gap analysis)
- that it serve as a tool where leadership candidates can compare their expectations with their host organization's expectations and core competence needs in order to be a successful leader in a learning organization
- that it document an individualized leadership development plan for each leader (and prospective leader) that is in line with the organization's strategic agenda

To be of real value, ILDPs must be part of a systematic process designed to solicit and identify the learning and development needs of leaders within the organization. It is a process where a leader and the organization make a commitment toward acquiring the necessary competence and KSAOCs important to the organization's success. And, it is a process where an organization makes a commitment toward providing the leader with a means of identifying and developing his or her current and future learning and development needs.

A key ingredient to the use of ILDPs is the standardization of events. This means that every leader must participate in measurable learning and development activities. Additionally, the overall ILDP process should accomplish the following:

1. Develop an ILDP oversight committee (possibly comprising leaders from different organizational levels and a HRD representative) to interpret the organization's strategic agenda into leadership development terms and manage the overall ILDP process (design, implementation, and evaluation).

2. Develop ILDPs for all current and future leaders.

3. Develop realistic job previews for all leadership jobs in the organization and make this information available to all relevant employees.

4. Ensure completion of 360 degree evaluations of all leaders based on key performance dimensions linked to the strategic imperatives of the organization. This information is used to formulate an ILDP.

5. Assign each leader an ILDP coach and develop an individualized ILDP plan.

6. Have the ILDP oversight committee review each ILDP plan and make recommendations and suggestions for improvement.

7. Ensure ILDP coaches and leaders meet to review the final ILDP plan before implementation.

8. Ensure ILDP implementation begins with specifc learning and development activities, completion dates, and meeting dates between ILDP coaches and leaders to discuss progress (and the need to revise plans depending on organizational changes, such as in strategic direction).

9. Ensure the ILDP oversight committee meet to review progress toward achievement of each ILDPs goals (i.e, at least every six months) and assess the overall program based on established evaluation criteria.

10. Generate regular reports for senior leadership by the ILDP oversight committee on the ILDP program to keep them up to date and to identify needed changes in the program.

ILDP Contingencies

As with many other development systems, the ILDP process should be time limited. Given the challenging demands on today's organizations, their leaders should be expected to work toward achieving their individual and group learning and development goals within a specified time frame. However, the time frame for a leader's development is most dependent on the current business demands which the leader, his or her supervisor, the ILDP coach, and the ILDP oversight committee must not lose sight of.

It should be easy to see that the ILDP process requires ongoing communication to be successful. Because the system is built on providing a leader with continuous feedback and communication on leadership expectations, and on how well they are meeting those expectations, everyone must work to ensure that poor communication does not hinder the success of the ILDP process.

An effective ILDP process is systematic and aimed at getting the most information about a leader and the learning and development needs and opportunities important to their own and the organization's success to the right people at the right time. The ILDP is not meant to intimidate the leader; rather, the ILDP should provide each leader with the comfort that their organization is committed 100 percent to providing developmental opportunities for them throughout their tenure in the organization.

CONCLUSION

All organizations engage in various forms of leadership development efforts, and at present many organizations have developed programs geared to help leaders better meet their total responsibilities. This chapter suggests that organizations are beginning to establish a new leadership development paradigm, one that is committed to improving leaders and better meeting the organization's strategic agenda.

ILDPs can improve the effectiveness and success of such efforts. The ILDP process affords employees with information about what successful leadership is about in their own and in other organizations, given a specific strategic agenda. In conclusion, the ILDP process highlighted in this chapter can help organizations to ensure that their leadership development efforts are (1) directed toward helping both organizations and employees meet their needs; (2) undertaken only when they are the most effective way to meet these needs; (3) solidly designed, using the latest state of the art; and (4) carefully administered and thoroughly evaluated.

CHAPTER 6

Enhancing Transfer of Training through Debriefing

Experiential learning exercises (ELEs) are an accepted and important part of most organizational training efforts. By their very nature, an ELE is a complex event. It needs to provide learners with the basis for understanding why and how the new knowledge and skills they acquire is related to what they already know. It must convey to the learners that they have the capability of using this new knowledge not only when they learn it in training, but also in their back-home work settings.

When rigorously administered, ELEs can be a powerful form of training and development in which participants acquire new KSAOCs through guided practice. Of crucial importance is the often neglected processing stage of an experiential learning exercise known as *debriefing*. Debriefing is the processing of the learning experience from which the learners are to draw the lessons to be learned (Lederman 1992; Thatcher 1986).

Effectively utilizing a debriefing process is based on two assumptions. First, the participation experience has influenced the participants in some meaningful way. Second, a processing (often a discussion, but this chapter will suggest other forms) of that experience is necessary to provide insight into that experience and its impact (Lederman 1992).

Debriefing should be an integral part of any experience-based learning activity. The main function of the debriefing phase of ELEs is to integrate experiences with learning and application transferable to participants' work settings. The trainer's role is to guide the participants in transforming some of the generalizations into more precise behaviors that can be applied to the "real world."

Unfortunately, in many instances those responsible for implementing training learn to debrief by debriefing. They seem to turn their attention more to the design and implementation of experientially oriented training activities (i.e., simulations or games) and the training effectiveness of them than to the same questions about the design, implementation, or debriefing assessment important to the success of such activities.

This chapter will focus on the process of debriefing and the postexperience analysis in the training setting. The chapter provides a conceptual model for debriefing based upon Kolb's (Kolb, Osland, & Rubin 1995) experiential learning model introduced in Chapter 3 and offers practical ideas for applying the model to debriefing. Special attention is also given to the role of the trainer in providing the environment necessary for a richer experience. The importance of the trainer's role in providing structure versus ambiguity is also addressed. This chapter will also offer general and specific guidelines for the conduct of ELEs and participant feedback which training and development professionals can use during the design, implementation, and debriefing of ELEs.

DEBRIEFING DEFINED AND PLANNING

Many writers agree that the literature on the process of debriefing is scarce (Lederman 1992; Wagenheim & Gemmill 1994). It is not surprising then that the debriefing practice also lacks the basis of conceptual models of systematic and analytical process. A debriefing process, however, must be planned as rigorously as the exercise itself to complete the learning experience.

While a number of authors write about the debriefing process, not all use the term "debriefing" to mean the same thing. Lederman (1992) notes that debriefing is variously defined as learning through reflection on a simulated experience (Lederman & Stewart 1986; Thatcher & Robinson 1990); emotional recovery from critical incidents (Bergmann & Queen 1987; Walker 1990); work-related tasks, such as appraisal and synthesis of input from focus groups (De Nicola 1990) or job performance (Bailey 1990).

The earliest documentation of debriefing is after military campaigns and war games (Pearson & Smith 1986). After a mission or exercise, the participants were brought together to describe and account for the activity, and to develop new strategies and tactics as a result of the exercise. More recently we have learned about debriefings of prisoners of war, hostages, and other crisis victims (Walker 1990). Not only do we gain information about their experiences but we also gain insight for those who were not there. In war or hostage trauma usage, the debriefing involves getting them to tell the story and describe their feelings. Similarly, in the training setting, participants also tell their story and describe their feelings. Clearly, however, both experiences are substantially different.

Another use of debriefing is in psychological studies involving the deception of subjects. In these studies the subjects have been deceived into doing something in an experiential context (Tennen & Gillen 1979). The purpose of debriefing in this scenario is to provide information rather than to gather information. To debrief them is to inform them (American Psychological Association 1979); to reverse laboratory induced experiences (Tennen & Gillen 1979); or to undo negative consequences, inform, and educate, and to check on the method used (Mills 1976). In the context of deception studies, debriefing is often synonymous with dehoaxing (Walker 1990).

Note that in the educational setting it is advisable to avoid deception (Warrick et al. 1979). For example, planting a disruptive person in a group to generate the desired result may create distrust and may sensitize the participants to look for gimmicks in future exercises. Another form of deception is the choice of exercises that may cause intergroup tensions that cannot be repaired. For example, prisoners' dilemmas or some power exercises may alienate groups from one another or the trainer for the remainder of the learning experience.

The debriefing stage must be planned so that it provides the learner with continuity of experience, as opposed to learning loss on the part of the participants due to a lack of experiencing and understanding its application to their work. For the experience to be maximally effective for learners, the debriefing must be allocated an adequate amount of time, or much of the potential richness of the experience is lost. No exact amount of time for the debriefing is recommended; the trainer can decide on the length of the debriefing session. Some of the factors training personnel should consider when determining the length of the debriefing session include purpose, complexity and level of intensity of the exercise; responsiveness of the participants; and format of the debriefing session (e.g., collaborative discussion or debriefing game, as discussed later).

A CONCEPTUAL MODEL FOR DEBRIEFING

In pursuit of achieving a level in which learners not only absorb the knowledge presented but also apply this learning in practice, it is helpful to consider the entire process of learning, and then to apply this learning process specifically to the debriefing session. Kolb's model of adult learning (Kolb, Osland, & Rubin 1995) defines each stage of the learning process and is presented in Table 6.1 for application to debriefing.

For each stage, key questions are provided which may help the facilitator progress through the stages by applying each to the debriefing. Additional questions are offered by Gaw (1979).

Though participants in the training initiative may naturally proceed through some of the stages in Kolb's ELM during a debriefing exercise, often the progression does not result in active experimentation (doing). For example, the trainer's goal may be to ultimately motivate a participant to use recently learned or acquired KSAOCs in new situations, yet some participants may merely conceptualize and not change practice, while others may try different methods of practice without integrating learned concepts and theories in a meaningful fashion. Through applying Kolb's model to the debriefing session, however, the trainer can guide learners through the stages to achieve active experimentation.

The goal of ELEs in training is for participants to engage in active experimentation. This is the phase of exploration that takes the participant from their own individual experience to the broader application of that experience to actual work situations. This stage is comparable to Lederman's (1992) phase of generalization and application. It is worth noting, however, that a number of activities to which Lederman refers broaden the generalization and application process; for example, she includes expressing feelings (Nissen & Ransom 1983), clarifying facts, concepts, or principles, assessing individual performance (Thatcher 1986), and recapping achievement (Pearson & Smith 1986).

What should occur during the application and transfer stage seems more clearly found in the active experimentation stage as described by Kolb (Kolb, Osland, & Rubin 1995). The focus in the debriefing is to influence people in an active way and to transform situations in a dramatic fashion. It emphasizes practical applications as opposed to reflective understanding, a pragmatic concern with what works as opposed to what is abstract, and an emphasis on doing as opposed to observing. Here, the focus is on getting things accomplished and achieving objectives. Impact and influence on the environment are valued. Active experimentation allows for testing the implications of concepts in new situations. These hypotheses are tested on future action, which in turn leads to new experiences.

Providing continuity of the learning experience (i.e., transfer of learning) is necessary and can be achieved by proceeding through all the stages in Kolb's model. It leads learners to understand the relationships between what they are currently learning, and past and future experiences. The richness and strength of the experiential learning exercise can be enhanced if debriefing proceeds through all of the stages of Kolb's model: from concrete experience to reflective observation to abstract conceptualization and ultimately to active experimentation.

Table 6.1
Debriefing Using the Kolb Model

Stage in Kolb's Model of the Learning Process	Description of Kolb's Stage	Questions for Application of Learning Stage to Stages in Debriefing Session
CONCRETE EXPERIENCE (*Feeling*)	The participants objectively describe the experience in terms of who, what, when, where, how. They also subjectively describe their feelings, perceptions, and thoughts that occurred *during* (not after) the experience. They tell their story.	*Did you or your team complete the assignment?* *Were the objectives of the assignment clear?* *How did you feel?*
REFLECTIVE OBSERVATION (*Watching*)	At this level, the experience is viewed from different participant's points of view which add more meaning and perspectives to the event. This approach values patience, impartiality, and considered, thoughtful judgment.	*Did you make assumptions about X, Y, Z?* *What was happening for you during the exercise?* *What did you observe in others?* *What did the exercise mean for you and in relation to others? (Clarify differences of opinion).*
ABSTRACT CONCEPTUALIZATION (*Thinking*)	The debriefing relates concepts from the readings and lecture to the experience in the activity. An original model or theory can be created.	*What work-related policies/rules could you make based on your experience in this exercise?* *With what situations would the rules/policies not apply?* *Given such situations, what would be a better rule/policy?*
ACTIVE EXPERIMENTATION (*Doing*)	The participants apply what has been learned in the experience of the activity to back home work situations. "What if" scenarios may be explored.	*How would you change aspects of the experience for a better outcome?* *In what situations could this strategy be utilized?* *What situations would call for a backup or different strategy?*

Source: Adapted from D. A. Kolb, J. S. Osland, & I. M. Rubin. 1995. *Organizational Behavior: An Experiential Approach*. 6th ed. Englewood Cliffs, NJ: Prentice Hall.

THE ROLE OF THE TRAINER IN DEBRIEFING

Equally important to the effective planning of a debriefing exercise is providing an environment that is conducive to completing the entire learning experience. It will be helpful to the trainer to understand the difference between the need for ambiguity and the need for structure in the exercise. Finally, providing ground rules in which participants will be able to experience all phases is helpful for keeping the session focused and effective. Both are described in the following section.

Encouraging an Environment of Ambiguity

As mentioned earlier, in spite of the efforts of those who design and implement training efforts, KSAOCs gained from an ELE will differ for some participants; thus, the debriefing session has the potential to be perceived with some degree of ambiguity. A certain amount of ambiguity is necessary so that participants are personally *stretched* to apply learning to their back home work situations. It may seem paradoxical that the pursuit of a conceptual model for debriefing is urged, when ambiguity is urged to meet the subjective needs of individuals. Both structure and ambiguity, however, can be met if the trainer is cognizant of each of the steps of the debriefing model, and uses it as a road map to facilitate discussion so that all learning stages are experienced.

When adult learners reach the level of active experimentation (doing), they will use new skills, having experienced their usefulness and meaningfulness, and will feel capable of using the skills, having experienced the competency to do so (Bandura 1977; Kolb, Osland, & Rubin 1995). The challenge for the trainer is to encourage the necessary amount of ambiguity so that learners can apply new KSAOCs in practice. The facilitator must provide guidance by assisting participants in keeping focused and effectively translating abstract conceptualization (theory) into active experimentation (practice).

This is similar to the notion of self efficacy in Bandura's social learning theory where human beings acquire new skills vicariously. Bandura (1977) argues that human beings think about and interpret their experiences, as opposed to absorbing blindly. From self-directed learning experiences, one gains a sense of self efficacy, in which new skills are used because the individual has experienced their usefulness and meaningfulness and feels capable of using the skills, having experienced the competency to do so. The trainer must encourage individuals to "give" and to "get" so they develop their own meaningful applications of their learning and will be more likely to experience their usefulness in actual work settings.

To provide ambiguity, it is necessary to create an environment of *mutuality* (a two-sided exchange), where learning is *self-directed*. Though there is no set method of creating such an environment, it may be helpful for the trainer to consider the alternatives to a lecture-oriented environment, which is typically one-sided, where trainers give and participants get. Adult learning needs are best fulfilled in an environment conducive to two-sided exchange. As Kolb states, in adult learning both giving and getting are critical. In getting, there is the opportunity to incorporate new ideas and perspectives. In giving, there is the opportunity to integrate and apply these new perspectives and to practice their use (1991, 58).

As a general rule, Thiagarajan (1992) recommends that the facilitator (trainer) take on a cooperative role (as opposed to hierarchical or autonomous), in which the balance of power is equal between facilitator and participants. This mutuality allows for the fulfillment of the "contract of reciprocity" (Kolb, Osland, & Rubin 1995), where learners take an active role, responsibility and interest for their learning.

Finally, in line with Gunz's view, trainers should provide a great deal of tutorial (or coaching) support (1995). A tutor with a good understanding of the exercise can ask appropriate questions of the participants, guiding them to appropriate observations from which they can build more helpful hypotheses. If this is not done, there is a risk that learners will not make any successful circuits of the Kolb cycle, and learning will not take place.

Providing Structure for the Exercise . . . the "Game Plan"

Once the format for the debriefing session (i.e., discussion, game, or constructive feedback) has been decided on, the trainer should consider explaining the game plan and ground rules for the session to the participants. By game plan, what is meant is a specific description of events and the timing of them during the debriefing session. In terms of the game plan, the trainer may choose to describe the game or discussion format to the group and how it will occur in the context of the stages. For example, if a constructive feedback session is used within the framework of Kolb's model, the trainer could describe that the experience will be discussed (concrete experience), followed by feedback from group members (reflective observation), followed by a conceptualization of rules that may apply to other situations (abstract conceptualizations), and concluded with practical applications of the KSAOCs to work situations (active experimentation). In describing the stages, the trainer can set a time limit for discussing each to ensure that there is ample time for all stages. If the group becomes lost in a digression, the trainer can refocus the debriefing by redirecting the group back to the game plan that had been previously articulated. The trainer can ensure focus by asking the types of questions for each stage provided earlier. Using this, the trainer has a tool for guiding the experiential learning cycle at the pace, depth, breadth, and intensity that seems appropriate.

Following the explanation of the game plan, setting *ground rules* for the debriefing session is important since it will involve discussing the actions of others, especially during the concrete experience (feeling) stage. Specifically, the trainer should convey that feedback should be descriptive (as opposed to evaluative), nonjudgmental and noncritical. The constructive (as opposed to destructive) purpose of the exercise must be underscored (Borisoff & Victor 1989). The next section offers suggestions useful to trainers for implementing ELEs.

PRACTICAL SUGGESTIONS FOR IMPLEMENTING ELEs

The goal of the ELE is to ensure that it has provided valuable learning that is practical for the individual. Similarly, in an effort to assist in the application of debriefing learning, the following suggestions for implementation are offered.

Shared Work Experiences

Participants discuss scenarios from their work experience in which the newly acquired learning would have been and will be helpful.

Instructions: Start the exercise by asking questions relevant to the concrete experience and reflective observation stages. During the abstract conceptualization and active experimentation stages, invite participants to share previous or potential work experiences in which the KSAOCs learned would have been or will be beneficial. For example, in the abstract conceptualization stage ask the following: Think about work experiences you have had that are similar to the situation you experienced in the exercise. Based on both experiences, what rule could you follow that would be beneficial to both situations? In the active experimentation phase ask, Can you think of other work situations in which this rule would apply? How about situations in which it would not apply? In situations where it would not apply, what would be a second alternative?

What this exercise achieves: It brings to life the concepts learned, and offers practical data for analysis (concrete experience) and ideas for applying theories and concepts (abstract conceptualization). This exercise encourages active experimentation.

The Envelope Game

Each group has the opportunity to explore what might have occurred during the exercise given different variables. Each group's questions are answered by other groups, inviting views from diverse prospectives. This exercise provides the grist for lively discussion (Thiagarajan 1992).

Instructions: Start the exercise by asking questions relevant to the concrete experience and reflective observation stages. During the abstract conceptualization and active experimentation stages, learners are divided into groups. Each group passes around an envelope which contains a "what if" exercise question, which is written on the outside of the envelope. Groups collaboratively answer the questions of other groups on paper (based on their experience and learning) which are then inserted in the appropriate envelope. As group responses are read, rules are formulated and summarized on a chalk board to engage learners in the abstract conceptualization stage. The trainer can then conclude with a discussion of the rules and how they apply to work and other settings (both from the resulting "what if" scenarios and other resulting discussion).

What this exercise achieves: It invites many different questions, which helps to personalize the learning. It provides ideas for work practice from many different perspectives that may not have otherwise been discussed. This exercise provides an opportunity for active experimentation.

Collaborative Discussion

Participants openly discuss each other's performance during various activities.

Instructions: During the concrete experience stage, the trainer asks participants to use the rules or guidelines of constructive feedback (discussed later in this chapter) to describe their performance. Program participants are then invited to offer feedback on the performance of others in the same fashion. Finally, the trainer synthesizes comments to provide transferrable ideas for practice (Klepper 1994).

What this exercise achieves: It helps participants to view their behavior and that of others objectively, and helps participants conceptualize the experiences from the learning exercise from many different perspectives. It provides a guideline for participants to evaluate real world situations and apply the KSAOCs learned, thus encouraging active experimentation.

Journal Writing

Participants record their experience, the relevant theories and concepts and their future application.

Instructions: After the learning exercise is completed, the trainer instructs participants to write about the experience in a journal. A general guideline for journal entries might be

1. Experience—Explain what happened during the exercise. Include your observations of others and how you felt about these interactions.

2. Theory or Model—Based on the readings, program lecturettes, and discussions, what theories apply or would be helpful to implement in the exercise?

3. Application—Considering the objectives of the exercise and your performance, how could you change the experience for a better outcome? How do you think the outcome would have changed and why? In what work situations could this strategy be utilized? What work situations could call for a backup strategy?

The trainer could then provide individual feedback on participants' journals. (*Note*: Depending on the format of the exercise, time limitations will dictate whether writing will occur before or after the exercise. Journal writing is an effective method of debriefing, and may be creatively utilized within training initiative format and time constraints.)

What this exercise achieves: Writing allows for uninhibited expression, the opportunity to reexamine written ideas, and to proceed through all learning stages in a structured manner. It also provides the opportunity for the trainer to comment and enhance each individual's needs and goals (Klepper 1994; Petranek, Corey, & Black 1992).

The successful implementation of ELEs by trainers can be increased by following some specific guidelines. These guidelines are discussed in the next section.

GUIDELINES FOR THE EFFECTIVE CONDUCT OF ELEs

Guidelines for the effective conduct of ELEs begins with a clear understanding of the realities of experiential learning. Experiential learning is rewarding and rigorous. It is fun and frustrating. It is exciting and exhausting. And, something will usually go wrong. Like many involved in the training profession and the field of experiential learning, I believe Murphy's Law was created by the first author of ELEs. There is a guideline for this problem: prepare, prepare, prepare. And in reality with all this preparation, experience has shown that one should still expect something to go wrong.

Since the objective of many ELEs is to encourage high participant involvement, it is important to clarify the trainer's role in facilitating participation as an important first step to establishing guidelines for conducting ELEs. Successful experientially based learning and its accompanying activities requires a somewhat different role for the trainer than does the nonexperiential standard lecture or seminar format.

In the nonexperiential learning format, the trainer assumes primary responsibility for the learning process. The objective of the learning process in the nonexperiential learning training initiative, course, or exercise is the assimilation of information and transfer of learning. The role of the trainer is to facilitate participant learning through various methods. The role of the participants in this process is to acquire the learning and think of how they will successfully transfer it to their back-home work situations.

In contrast, the role of the trainer in experiential learning-oriented training initiatives and specific ELEs is to create a learning environment in which participants are motivated to find answers to their questions, organizational challenges, problems, issues, and opportunities. Trainers are just as involved as their instructor–trainer counterparts, but their involvement is very different. Trainers are equally concerned with process and content. Participants are actively involved in the process and are expected to link exercise learning to their work situations.

Enthusiasts are convinced that in some circumstances, and for some forms of learning, experiential learning can be a strategy that is more powerful and economically viable than any other. On the other hand, critics argue that experiential learning is always of doubtful value because its results are impossible to evaluate, can sometimes be counterproductive to learning, and in any case, is unnecessarily time-consuming. Between these two extremes fall many in training who would like to "give experiential learning a go" but often complain that they are unable to find suitable exercises and guidelines for conducting the exercises.

With this as a backdrop, the implicit message of the guidelines offered here are that it is not only the ELE, but what you do with it, that counts. The best practices presented in the following section should serve as guidelines for conducting ELEs (general and specific) and participant feedback in training efforts.

Best Practices in Conducting ELEs: General Guidelines

ELEs should provide sufficient opportunities for the participants to learn and ensure that participants are highly involved in discussion and practice activities.

The participant must be involved in the process. Experiential learning is active rather than passive. Rather than only listening to lectures, participants must do role plays, make decisions (as in a simulation game or other experientially oriented exercise), or perform an analysis of an organization's problems.

The ELE should be interactive. The interaction involves more than just the trainer–participant dyad. Participant–participant, participant–client, or participant–environment interaction is also required.

ELEs should take a whole person emphasis. Such exercises should involve learning in the behavioral and affective dimensions as well as the cognitive dimensions. Given the problem-solving orientation of many management development efforts, there is a natural tendency by trainers to emphasize the cognitive dimension. However, given the importance of "people skills" and "technical skills" in most organizations, the broader horizons offered by experiential learning approaches may be very beneficial. The development of a participant's interpersonal and other cognitive skills is one of the major expected benefits from experiential learning.

The term "experience" implies a "real-world" contact (or at least "real-world" like) contact. Participants should be exposed to real or simulated environment experiences that are analogous to the real situations that participants currently face or will face later. Participants should be provided with a variety of situations. Since different participants will react quite differently to the same situational cue, the interaction process should be monitored closely.

Trainers should maintain variety in introducing and using ELEs. They should use different approaches for introducing ELEs, and where appropriate, adapt the exercises to the participant's learning needs, interests, and learning styles.

Trainers should select experiential learning exercises for a particular program or course wisely, and experiment with various combinations and sequences.

ELEs should be closely linked to enhancing the development of KSAOCs and competency levels important to achieving organizational results.

All ELEs should be structured and monitored. If there is insufficient autonomy, the willingness to participate may be greatly stifled. On the other hand, if there is no guidance provided, the experience may be largely meaningless in terms of the specific content area for which the trainer is responsible. An ELE by itself will not insure learning; the trainer has to insure that it is a quality experience.

Trainers should ask provocative questions rather than providing impressive answers. Therefore, the trainer's planning notes should be organized around a series of questions and learning outcomes rather than a logical outline of the material.

Best Practices in Conducting ELEs: Specific Conduct

Trainers should decide in advance why they want to use each ELE for a particular course, group, or learning outcome. There are four factors that trainers need to take into account when they look for and decide on an ELE:

1. What do you want the participants to get out of it (learn)?

2. What does the organization want participants to get out of it (learn)?

3. What will be the form or structure of the exercise design?

4. Who are the participants?

ELEs should have the expected learning outcomes articulated and related to the overall curriculum. Experiences occurring without guidance and adequate preparation may yield little insight into the general processes taking place.

Trainers should take as much time as they need to explain the exercise (especially when using games or simulations), and ask and answer questions to ensure the learning outcomes, rules, and roles are understood. When role playing exercises are used, the trainers should give the role players any guidelines they need for action within the ELE's represented setting.

During the introduction phase of an ELE the trainer should set the stage for upcoming activities in terms of the following questions: Where have we been? Where are we going? How are we going to get there? Participants will appreciate an organized learning experience, and given the initial resistance many have toward ELEs, providing a conceptual road map or agenda for each exercise (and session) helps participants find order amongst the seeming chaos.

Trainers should next focus participants' attention on specific learning objectives and on their work-related results and KSAOCs.

After the completion of the introduction, the trainer should initiate the ELE (or series of brief activities).

Depending on the ELE, the trainer's role will vary from active to passive. The trainer should be prepared to explain her or his actions to participants at all times.

Afterward, in debriefing, the trainer should allow the group (or each participant) to take responsibility for its (or her or his) own conclusions, which will be based on their own direct or indirect experience (or observers, such as the trainer, when they are used in the ELE).

At the conclusion of ELEs, discussion should focus on

1. What have we learned?

2. How does this relate to the key learning outcomes introduced at the beginning of the initiative, course, day, or exercise?

3. How will we take what we've learned and apply it to related work experiences, problems, or opportunities back on the job?

During debriefing, the trainer should be prepared to move in and out of the discussion to help participants relate their conclusions, ideas, concerns, or learnings to their existing KSAOCs and work experiences. The trainer should monitor this discussion carefully, be alert to correct any mistakes of fact (assuming that the group does not do so), add more information when necessary, offer examples and suggestions, ask constructive questions in order to enlarge discussion (or debate when appropriate), encourage group problem solving, and enhance group learning from the ELEs.

During debriefing, the trainer should insure the integration of the experiences with KSAOCs and applications to relevant work situations so that appropriate generalizations and potential applications can be made.

During debriefing, the trainer should encourage participants to exchange feedback and clarify strengths and weaknesses in their interpersonal behavior.

During debriefing, the trainer should direct attention to both the content and process of the ELE with respect to both conceptual and personal learning.

Debriefing should be behaviorally oriented and should focus on the relationships that developed.

Throughout an ELE, the trainer should be prepared to move continually from an active to passive role, or from task minded to people minded.

Ongoing participant evaluations of ELEs should be encouraged, and information from those evaluations should be used to improve ELEs (i.e., participant learning). Allowing for such ongoing feedback allows for modifications in ELEs where appropriate. This feedback is often dynamic in nature and can serve as a reality check as to whether participants understand and can articulate and apply learning to their back-home work situations.

In summary, since the trainer is often the person ultimately responsible for choosing and facilitating ELEs, their behavior is important in determining what kind of learning the participants derive from the whole training initiative and particular ELEs. It is true that in all training techniques or methods the personality of the trainer is critical, which is why no two trainers are interchangeable, no matter how similar their backgrounds or experiences. However, whenever an ELE is the learning strategy, guidelines for conducting the exercise are as vital and important an ingredient as the trainer's leadership style.

Best Practices in Conducting Participant Feedback

Providing feedback to participants during debriefing (and training overall) is a key component to successful ELEs. The link between objectives, course materials, and the ELEs seems rarely, if ever, crystal clear to the participants. In the organizational world, this is even more relevant because some training audiences resist ELEs, as suggested earlier. Adequate attention must be given to feedback and the debriefing process in particular. Trainers must be competent in providing feedback, managing the feedback process between participants, and debriefing the experiential exercises. Such competence allows trainers to better assist the participants in receiving and giving constructive feedback, processing learning information from exercises, and making real-life, on-the-job applications. It is incumbent upon trainers that they see their role in the feedback and debriefing process as one of helping participants to see the linkages to their own real-life, back-at-work experiences and possible future career situations.

Participant feedback and the debriefing process are major opportunities for participant learning. As noted earlier, the main function of the trainer during the debriefing process is to insure an integration of the ELEs with KSAOCs and applications to participant work situations, so that the appropriate generalizations can be made. It is also important that the trainer encourages participants to exchange feedback and clarify strengths and weaknesses important to success in the organization.

Giving feedback in ELEs should be analogous to holding up a mirror where individuals can see themselves as others see them and learn how their actions have been affecting others. It is not telling others what is wrong with them nor telling them how they *should* change. Trainers and participants should recognize that feedback is offering their perceptions and describing their feelings in a nonjudgmental manner that data recipients can use as they find appropriate.

Trainers should find the following guidelines useful when providing feedback to participants:

1. When giving feedback, providers should consider the needs of the person receiving the feedback, as well as their own. Feedback providers should ask themselves what they want the individual to get out of the information. Feedback should genuinely attempt to improve performance or the relationship instead of "dumping."

2. Providers of feedback should examine their own motives. They should be sure their intentions are to be helpful, not to show how perceptive and superior they are, or to hurt the other. Be on the other person's side.

3. Providers of feedback should consider the receiver's readiness to hear their feedback. In general, feedback is most useful when it is sought, rather than when it is volunteered. When possible, wait for signs of the other wanting it.

4. Feedback should be given promptly. Feedback given soon after the event, except when the individual is upset or otherwise not ready to listen, is better than that given when details are no longer clear in anyone's mind.

5. Confrontational feedback should be avoided and only used in extreme cases (i.e., issues of safety, integrity, or in instances where participants may be exhibiting inappropriate behavior, such as providing destructive versus constructive feedback to other participants).

6. Feedback should not be given in the form of advice that can be interpreted as helping a participant make a nonwork-related personal decision or other decisions that are better left to discussion with a trained professional.

7. Trainers and participants should not give any feedback that places them in the position of a professional expert (i.e, counselor, psychologist, psychotherapist, or psychiatrist).

8. Feedback should deal in specifics, not generalities. Feedback given to participants by the trainer or other participants should always be specific and behaviorally based. Describe concrete events ("You interrupted me when I was reviewing. . ." versus "You always try to hog all the air time").

9. Feedback should only be given on behaviors that are directly relevant to the exercise (or series of exercises) at hand and where there is evidence that the behavior is reflective of back-home behaviors exhibited by the participant.

10. Feedback providers should avoid *feedback overload*. The feedback should focus only on what is most important and changeable (behavior that the receiver can do something about).

11. Feedback should be *descriptive* rather than evaluative. The feedback should describe what the person did and any feelings it aroused in you (the giver), but avoid labels and judgments by describing rather than evaluating behavior. ("You interrupted me and that frustrates me because I lose track" is descriptive; "You were rude" is evaluative).

12. Feedback should be given using "I" statements as opposed to "you" statements to reduce defensiveness.

13. Feedback should focus on the impact of the behavior on the person giving it, the group in the exercise, and where possible, in the back-home work situation (this is especially important when intact workgroups are involved).

14. Feedback should be given in a calm, unemotional language, tone, and body language.

15. Feedback should be offered, not imposed. Feedback providers should give information as something the receiver can consider and explore, not as a command that he or she change.

16. Feedback should be offered in a *spirit of tentativeness*, as one person's perceptions, not as "the truth." Being dogmatic usually puts people on the defensive.

17. Feedback providers should be open to receiving feedback themselves. Feedback providers must recognize that their own actions may be contributing to the other's behavior; not everyone may feel the same about the other, which reflects on the feedback provider's perceptions, as well as on the other's behavior.

18. Feedback should highlight the costs of the receiver's behavior to the provider. Feedback providers should try to help the other person see how the behavior in question costs him or her or prevents meeting his or her objectives (learning or work).

19. Feedback providers should watch for any behavior of the other while receiving which confirms or disconfirms the feedback.

In summary, feedback to participants is a critical step in ELEs. The success of feedback depends largely on its ability to arouse individual and group action and to direct energy toward increased learning, problem solving, and transfer of learning. Whether feedback serves these energizing functions depends on the content of the feedback, and on the process by which they are fed back to participants. Trainers must understand that the characteristics of effective feedback pertain to its *content*, and should be relevant, understandable, descriptive, verifiable, limited, impactful, comparative, and unfinalized. In addition to the characteristics of the feedback, it is equally important for trainers to attend to the *process* by which that information is fed back to participants. Since people often come to ELEs with strong feelings ranging from excitement, anxiety, fear, and hope, trainers need to manage the feedback process so that constructive discussion and problem solving occur.

CONCLUSION

It is suggested in this chapter that debriefing is a necessary part of the experiential learning process, crucial to completing the training or learning experience. The literature neglects the subject of debriefing, and writers are not in agreement about what it means to debrief. Kolb's model (Kolb, Osland, & Rubin 1995) of the learning process is offered as a conceptual model for achieving the ultimate goal of active experimentation from the ELE.

Attention has also been given to the role of the trainer in the process. This individual must provide the environment in which learning can occur and be transferred to work situations. To meet these goals, structure is required. It is also necessary, however, that ambiguity is allowed so that learners can personalize the learning, experiencing meaningfulness in its application, where learning is truly relevant to the individual.

ELEs can be a powerful form of training in which participants actually utilize new KSAOCs in the workplace. It is urged that, to obtain the optimum payoff (active experimentation) from the ELE, close attention must be paid to debriefing. Reaching the level of active experimentation requires an approach based on a conceptual model of systematic and analytical debriefing which is as rigorously planned as the ELE itself.

Effective use of the guidelines for conducting ELEs and providing feedback to participants will increase the success of any training endeavor. In addition, the guidelines should enhance the transfer of learning from training by participants back to their work situations, which in the end is the true measure of training success.

CHAPTER 7

Training Evaluation

As the cost of doing business continues to increase and competition becomes more fierce, organizations are using training to build required KSAOCs, indoctrinate new employees, transform organizational culture, do more with fewer employees, merge new acquisitions into the organization, and build multiple skills for radically changing jobs. With the increased importance of training, and increased funding in some instances, accountability becomes a key issue in organizations as they want clear measurement of training's contribution to bottom-line goals. This need for increased accountability and training effectiveness should come as no surprise to anyone working in training. Since training does not always pay off in immediate performance improvements, it is extremely difficult to establish a cause-and-effect relationship. For training professionals, the ability to resolve this dilemma would reduce many problems (e.g., techniques or topical information not proving valuable could be deleted from future training sessions). Effective evaluation techniques would also allow trainers to improve training scientifically and demonstrate their contribution to the organization's bottom line. In effect, this capability would permit training executives to provide more evidence to top executives of their contribution to organization success.

For training personnel, this focus on the bottom line has meant undertaking more complex evaluations on a more frequent basis as they try to respond to questions regarding "what works," "impact on performance individual, team, and organizational performance," "return on investment (ROI)," and "effectiveness of employee and management training overall." It also has led to an emphasis on translating training outcomes into measurements that directly affect an organization's health and success, such as market share, productivity, gross income, percentage of sales, customer satisfaction, or repeat business.

This chapter is the first of two chapters on the evaluation of training. This chapter will first discuss several reasons for the lack of training evaluation, in order to examine myths and barriers to training evaluation. Next, the chapter focuses on the objectives and benefits of training evaluation. The chapter concludes with a discussion of design options for training evaluation. Chapter 8 will discuss the when, how, and what of training evaluation.

WHY TRAINING EVALUATION DOESN'T OCCUR

Because training is an important variable in achieving an organization's strategic objectives, the effectiveness of training and the ability to measure its impact is increasingly imperative. However, as mentioned earlier, evaluating the success of training is a critical, but still often neglected aspect of the process, and the reasons are numerous. For example, as unbelievable as it may seem in this day and age, many training personnel are unaware that they should conduct evaluations. This is unfortunate because it ultimately results in training initiatives that are less effective than might be the case, and it leaves their efforts (and themselves) open to heavy criticism from various stakeholders.

The concept of training evaluation has been widely received as beneficial, but the practice of evaluation has lagged behind (Sims 1993). Few reports of actual evaluation of training efforts have been published; compared to the number of training initiatives, few evaluations have been conducted. Lack of training evaluation is even more evident as organizations have taken a closer look at the training process and realized that it is possibly the least developed, yet it is arguably the most important. Despite the hundreds of articles, books, and seminars devoted annually to the topic, training evaluation remains largely misunderstood, neglected, or misused. Still too often training is done without any thought of measuring and evaluating how well the training worked. Yet, the training process is not complete until and unless evaluation has taken place, for it is evaluation which informs training and gives it meaning.

Clearly many organizations still have not implemented formal training evaluation procedures. And, very often organizations and their training personnel do not conduct formal evaluation programs because they believe it cannot be done (DeWine 1994). In line with discussion to this point, Phillips (1997, 2–4) has identified a variety of myths surrounding the evaluation of the training process that training professionals must overcome if they are to successfully implement evaluations:

Myth #1   I can't measure the results of my training efforts.

Myth #2   I don't know what information to collect.

Myth #3   If I can't calculate the return on investment, then it is useless to evaluate the program.

Myth #4   Measurement is only effective in the production and financial areas.

Myth #5   My chief executive officer does not require an evaluation, so why should I do it?

Myth #6   There are too many variables affecting behavior change for me to evaluate the impact of training.

Myth #7   Evaluation will lead to criticism.

Myth #8   I don't need to justify my existence because I have a proven track record.

Myth #9   The emphasis on evaluation should be the same in all organizations.

According to DeWine (1994), Myth #5 becomes a cover for many of the other excuses. If no one has asked for the information, why should I put myself through the extra trouble? Underlying Myths #1, #2, #6, and #7 is a lack of confidence or ability to conduct such evaluation programs. Therefore, excuses are invented about the kind of information to collect and the way in which to collect it. Myths #3 and #4 suggest very limited uses of evaluation programs, and thus provide an excuse for nonimplementation. Myth #8 may suggests a false sense of security. If the only reason someone can think of to conduct an evaluation is to justify his or her existence, then it probably does need to be justified.

In his 1996 book titled *Accountability in Human Resource Management*, Phillips discusses myths that have hindered human resources and training professionals from measuring their contribution, which also sheds additional light on why the adoption of sound evaluation practices have been slow in coming. The nine myths are as follows:

Myth #1   Evaluation should not be undertaken if the training staff is not motivated to pursue it.

Myth #2   Evaluation is difficult.

Myth #3   The least important training activities are measurable, while the most important training activities are not.

Myth #4   Evaluation is needed to justify the training function's existence.

Myth #5   There is no time for evaluation.

Myth #6   Evaluation is too expensive.

Myth #7   If top management does not require it, evaluation should not be pursued.

Myth #8   Unless a ROI is calculated, evaluation will be useless.

Myth #9   There are too many variables affecting training initiative performance to measure and evaluate the function.

As evidenced by the overlap of the two lists of myths, the problems connected to evaluating training may be reinforced by the larger training, HRD and HR cultures and their resistance to the evaluation process. In addition, training personnel must recognize that myths are not the only reasons evaluation of training is not performed. Many are very realistic and represent genuine barriers to an ongoing commitment to evaluating training as highlighted in the next section.

BARRIERS TO EVALUATING TRAINING

Wexley and Latham (1991) note that it is difficult to understand why the rigorous evaluation of training efforts is the exception rather than the rule. There are a number of reasons (Brethower & Rummler 1979; Grove & Ostroff 1990; Wexley & Latham 1991; Sims 1993; Dionne 1996; Phillips 1996) including the following:

1. *Evaluation of training means different things to different people.* There does not seem to be a consistent definition of what training evaluation is among HRD personnel.

2. *Top management does not usually require evaluation.* Frequently top management seems ready to take on faith that certain training initiatives are valuable. Moreover, top leaders reward their training staff for merely staying current with the latest training fads. When funding is good, top leadership appears to have no problem embracing the value of most training efforts. Further, when a needs analysis implies that training in certain areas is "good to do," it appears to be especially easy for top management to rest assured that things are being done properly by those responsible for training.

3. *There is no perceived need by those responsible for training.* It is easy for training personnel to believe that they have spent so much time and effort in, for example, design or usability studies, that it is clear the training effort works. They simply do not feel that evaluation needs to be done—a common and easy trap. Part of the problem is that it is not necessarily an explicit belief of which a person is aware. It is implicit, and only manifested by a variety of excuses, such as "It would just be a waste of time and money," "I would only find out what I already know," and so forth.

4. *Most senior-level training executives (and other staff) do not know how to go about evaluating training initiatives.* Evaluation of training is a complex procedure. Most people simply do not know how to evaluate training efforts properly.

5. *Senior-level training managers and staff do not know what to evaluate.* Many people are not clear on what questions should be answered by an evaluation. Should they focus on the number of key people who want to attend the program? The costs per trainee? The degree of enjoyment expressed by trainees? Changes back on the job? A major contributor to this problem is a lack of clear training objectives.

6. *The serious evaluation of training in organizations is a difficult task and is perceived as costly and risky.* There are two forces acting on training professionals that work against evaluation: cost and risk taking. Many training personnel would rather spend their limited funds on developing new and highly visible training offerings that hopefully will be seen favorably by top management, rather than spending scarce dollars on evaluation. The risk with evaluation is that the results may show that a training program that top management and others like is not attaining the objectives for which it was designed.

7. *Training personnel* do not *have the resources (i.e., time, money, or personnel).* This may be because they failed to include this item in the budget, budgets were cut, there were unforseen expenses, time ran short, or any other number of reasons.

8. *Training personnel (or clients)* perceive *that they do not have the resources.* For example, training personnel may move onto other "critical" projects that have a higher priority than evaluation of the project just completed. They could make the time, but they perceive that relative to other needs, they do not have the time (or money).

9. *Training personnel do not want to know.* Training personnel who champion a training initiative may feel threatened by the prospect of an objective evaluation of the initiative's effectiveness. Sometimes, unconsciously, training personnel simply do not want to know the results of a final evaluation. This is most often the case when they are consciously or unconsciously aware of the fact that they have had to make compromises; they have not had the resources or time to do the evaluation the way they would have liked. This reason for not performing an evaluation is almost always implicit, outside of our awareness.

10. *Attention to evaluation in the design of training initiatives.* The design, development, and implementation of training efforts have not always followed logical steps, leaving efforts to evaluate results futile and inconclusive.

11. *Lack of standards.* There is a lack of standards for judging the success of training efforts. Unfortunately, generally accepted evaluation standards have not been developed for the field of HR in general and for training in particular.

12. *A training effort changes hands.* The training design team delivers the initiative to an outside vendor (i.e., a company or academic institution), and then the training personnel are done with it, and it is now in the hands of another party. It becomes a question of ownership and responsibility. Who is responsible for determining the effectiveness of the training initiative? Often it is the client or outside vendor that receives the train-

ing program, who is implicitly responsible for doing the evaluation. But generally they don't feel that they should, they don't know how, or they don't have the time.

The following actions can be used by training personnel to counteract barriers to training evaluation (Wexley &Latham 1991; Sims 1993; Phillips 1996; Dionne 1996):

1. Make sure training is connected to a specific project, initiative, or result. It is often best to link training to a specific project and as close to roll-out as possible. Do just-in-time and results-based training.

2. To be effective, evaluation should be planned as one or more steps in program design. These steps should focus on planning the evaluation scheme, collecting data, analyzing data, interpreting the results, and communicating them to appropriate stakeholder audiences.

3. Top-level executives need to be educated on the importance of rigorous evaluation and the dangers of taking on faith that a certain training strategy is worthwhile.

4. Training managers and their staffs need to be taught the "how to's" of training evaluation. They need to be given hands-on training, where they are shown how to design questionnaires, use the correct experimental design, statistically analyze data, and calculate utility.

5. Training managers and top-level leadership need to discuss and determine what exactly needs to be evaluated and why. Training needs to be incorporated into the organization's strategic agenda. It is important that the organization's overall, HR, HRD, and training strategies are aligned.

6. If top management really wants to reinforce rigorous evaluation, they need to make it clear to the training officers or executives that a certain proportion of the training budget should be targeted to evaluation.

7. The risk-taking component of evaluation needs to be minimized by rethinking the purpose of evaluation. Rather than thinking of evaluation as a live or die decision for a training initiative, evaluation needs to be thought of as a way of finding out if there is anything wrong with the program, and if there is, correcting it.

8. Examine the cost of evaluation when compared to the perceived value derived from the process. In some cases, an evaluation may not be worth the added cost.

9. Develop and adopt acceptable performance measures, standards, and indices for training, and report the results publicly or through benchmarking projects.

A critical ingredient that should not be missing in any training function is a focus on continuous improvement. Past performance is no benchmark for the future, and training personnel must see the evaluation of training as a continuous improvement tool. However, as noted earlier in this chapter, in many instances training personnel may be too focused on the content of training, fixed training goals, and standards and tend to be more concerned with their performance compared with the past than their ability to evaluate their current training activities.

Those responsible for training make a fatal error if they persist in not taking a proactive approach in evaluating *all* of their training efforts; that is, those activities that fall under the umbrella of training should be perceived as moving targets that continuously stretch the training function to do better. The challenge to these training functions in organizations is to be sure that they are continuously updating their training efforts and performance. This keeps the emphasis on continuous improvement in training through evaluation where it should be.

The remainder of this chapter focuses on evaluation as an important stage of the training process. Training *evaluation* suggests change (or at least the potential for change) that promotes skepticism and criticism, and that seeks to establish (and question) relationships among training needs, objectives, and actions within an organization. As such, the evaluation of training programs, like the training itself, is derived from careful diagnosis and is meant to improve particular areas of individual and organizational functioning identified in that diagnosis.

In reality, evaluation is concerned with providing feedback to the training function and organizational members about the progress and impact of training efforts. Such information may suggest the need for further diagnosis and modification of the training initiatives, or it may show that the training efforts are successful. The next section discusses the objectives and benefits of training evaluation.

TRAINING EVALUATION OBJECTIVES AND BENEFITS

The primary and overriding objectives of the evaluation of training initiatives should be to collect data that will serve as a valid basis for improving the training system and maintaining quality control over its components. It must be emphasized that *all* components of the system and their interaction are the objects of scrutiny and that training personnel should ensure that training initiatives are designed with *a priori* consideration given to evaluation; that is, training personnel should be committed to evaluating the effectiveness of their initiatives. Several potential benefits result from evaluating training efforts are as follows:

1. Improved accountability and cost effectiveness for training initiatives which might result in an increase in resources.
2. Improved effectiveness (Are initiatives producing the results for which they were intended?).

3. Improved efficiency (Are the initiatives producing the results for which they were intended with a minimum waste of resources?).

4. Greater credibility for the training staff to include information on how to do a better job now or in future initiatives, or to redesign current or future initiatives.

5. Stronger commitment to and understanding of training by key executives and managers so they can make up for deficiencies and confirm or disconfirm subjective feelings about the quality of organizational training.

6. Formal corrective feedback system for developing strengths and weaknesses of training participants.

7. Trainees that understand the experience more fully and are more committed to the initiative.

8. Leaders better able to determine whether to send potential recruits to future training initiatives.

9. Quantifiable data for organizational researchers and training initiative developers interested in training research.

10. Increased visibility and influence for training initiative sponsors.

11. Increased knowledge and expertise in the development and implementation of training initiatives that produce the results for which they were intended.

This is not an exhaustive list of the objectives and benefits of evaluating training initiatives evaluation, however, training personnel who are responsible for training must continually ask themselves what the objectives of evaluation are and what they want to gain by conducting an evaluation.

A priori consideration of evaluation gives the training personnel at least five important advantages:

1. The ability to identify relevant audiences interested in training evaluation early in the process to ensure that evaluation feedback addresses their interests and information needs.

2. The development of an evaluation process that complements the training initiative. Evaluative methods can be carefully incorporated to minimize any disruptive effects on the training initiative.

3. The ability to construct a research design that allows for valid conclusions about the initiative's effectiveness. This includes finding appropriate premeasures, selecting appropriate groups or individuals to train, identifying comparison groups, and isolating extraneous variables prior to beginning training.

4. The ability to delineate material, data, and HR and HRD requirements for evaluation and incorporating these as part of the training initiative, not simply as an appendix to the training initiative.

5. The ability to modify the training initiative based on feedback gained through ongoing evaluation. Corrective feedback is crucial when modifying or upgrading subsequent stages of the training initiative.

Thus, training personnel committed to evaluation can enjoy benefits and advantages that have long been sacrificed in training designs without evaluation.

TRAINING EVALUATION RESOURCES AND CONSTRAINTS

Another important key to the success of training initiative evaluation depends on the extent to which the training staff can overcome problems through a methodologically sound design and implementation scheme. The evaluation plan should be developed through selection of alternatives assessed against the objectives of the evaluation and existing constraints and resources. A familiarity with available resources, imposing constraints, and methodological alternatives will allow accurate, useful, and practical training program evaluations.

Those responsible for designing and implementing training initiative evaluations in organizations must also pay particular attention to the availability of resources and constraints for such an endeavor. Resources are needed to evaluate training. Constraints can limit evaluation effectiveness. Both are considerations in selecting evaluation methods and procedures. For example, time is a constraint for most training evaluations and is often perceived as one of the major barriers to conducting training evaluations. The time available for collecting, analyzing, and reporting evaluation results is limited. This influences not only procedures for data collection and analysis, but also the type of data collected. Time may not permit development of tailored survey instruments for collecting reaction data, and training personnel may turn to alternatives such as off-the-shelf questionnaires. Such a decision may reduce evaluation time; however, the evaluator may be constrained to measure what the instrument purports to measure, rather than variables of interest. Some resources or constraints issues are

1. *Funding.* This refers to the dollars allotted to cover training evaluation planning and implementation.
2. *Time.* Evaluation can take place immediately or at periodic intervals after trainees return to the job. A sequence of "milestones" can be used. This includes completion of pretest and posttest data collection, data analysis, and dissemination of results to appropriate audiences.

3. *Human resources.* Trained personnel such as statisticians, computer specialists, research methodologists, and other trainers can be resources in evaluation.

4. *Organizational climate.* Evaluation is facilitated or hampered by the level of trust and openness of executives, managers, employees, or participants. Do people seek and are they receptive to evaluative feedback?

5. *Availability of data.* Evaluation is improved by the availability and quality of organizational information. Examples are records of individual, group, department and organization performance, reports, and personnel training records. Data can be obtained from surveys, interviews, and observations of employees.

6. *Details of the training evaluation action plan.* A good evaluation plan contains objectives, timetables, procedures, participants, locations, and possible use of strategies.

7. *Audiences.* The success of evaluation depends partly upon the information needs and interests of the key participants in the training process.

8. *Technical ability.* Evaluation requires the availability of standardized instruments, computerized analyses, stored data, logistics in collecting and disseminating results, and the abilities of persons involved.

9. *Ethical concerns.* Evaluations must recognize issues of privacy, employee and organizational confidentiality, obtrusiveness, and other harmful or illegal aspects of data collection and reporting.

To a large extent, these are interdependent factors to which the training staff must attend during the training initiative planning analysis.

TRAINING EVALUATION DESIGN OPTIONS

Upon identifying important training outcome criteria, the organization's training staff must select an experimental design to measure changes in these variables. The training staff has to make choices about how to design the evaluation of training to achieve valid results. The key question is how to design the evaluation to show whether training did in fact produce the observed results. This is called *internal validity*; the secondary question of whether training would work similarly in other situations is referred to as *external validity*.

Designing a good evaluation effort involves knowing when to collect evaluation measures and which groups to collect them from. Together, these factors determine the experimental design used to assess the impact of training. More specifically, the training evaluation design refers to the steps taken to ensure that (1) a change occurred (e.g., employee productivity increased or accidents declined); (2) the change can be attributed to the training effort; and (3) that a similar change could be expected if the training were done again with other employees.

Of course, the ability to make such statements will depend on the experimental rigor incorporated in the training evaluation process. Conclusive statements about the effectiveness of training can be made only when the trainer strictly adheres to experimental principles such as manipulation of variables, random assignment, control of extraneous and/or confounding variables, and equivalence of groups. Unfortunately, conducting experimentation in the field has proven to be a difficult, almost overwhelming, task. Many organizations generally demand that all employees in a department be trained, not only those randomly selected. It is also difficult for training personnel to control the many variables that can affect a worker's job behavior at a given time (e.g., interaction with coworkers or a supervisor, personal relationships, promotions). However, previous training evaluations have been able to overcome these difficulties by using several highly effective designs for evaluating training.

Numerous research designs can be used to evaluate the effectiveness of training. The more rigorous the design, the more confidence can be placed in the assertion that changes in learning, behavior, and results are due to the program (Kirkpatrick 1996).

A simple design is the *one-group baseline and "after" design*, in which one group of participants in the program is assessed before and after the experience. The differences in the baseline and "after" measures may be due to the training, or there may be a "Hawthorne effect"— that is, the employees conclude that they are being studied, so they work harder than usual. There is also the probability that over time, employees gain experience and acquire ways to do the job better. Self-development may have nothing to do with the training initiative. The baseline and "after" one-group design doesn't address the Hawthorne effect or natural improvements due to experience.

A research design that addresses the Hawthorne effect and the effect of experience is a two-group design. One group receives the training, while the other group receives no training. This design is an improvement over the one-group design, but we do not know if the groups were comparable to begin with. Perhaps the no-training group initially included significantly better performers. Since no baseline measures were taken, the conclusions drawn are somewhat debatable.

A two-group baseline measure is better than the one group design or the no-baseline two-group design. It permits the researcher to conclude with some confidence that differences in the criteria (i.e., learning or behavior) may be attributable to the training (and development) initiative.

Regardless of the design selected, training personnel must adhere to certain basic experimental principles. First, when possible, both pretest and posttest data should be collected on relevant criteria. Second, selection of participants should be randomized when possible. If it is not possible, solid quasi-experimentation should be employed. Third, reliability of data collected should be monitored throughout the evaluation. Fourth, when statistical analyses are performed, characteristics of the sample and data should conform to the assumptions of tests used. Finally, the evaluation process (i.e., training, data collection, and implementation) should be conducted in a manner to allow valid inferences about the effectiveness of training.

The final success of the training initiative evaluation depends on how well the training personnel and others can overcome problems through a methodologically sound design and implementation scheme. The evaluation plan should be developed through selection of alternatives assessed against the objectives of the evaluation and existing constraints and resources. A familiarity with available resources, imposing constraints, and methodological alternatives will allow accurate, useful, and practical training program evaluations.

TRAINING EVALUATION CHECKLIST

Improvements in employee performance and achievement of organizational results are the goals of the evaluation of training outcomes. A checklist of such a process that training personnel can use to evaluate the results of training might include the following:

1. Does the evaluation design fit the objectives of the training initiative?
2. Does the design address important issues such as initiative participants' needs and expectations? (These include both process and content issues.)
3. Does the evaluation method reflect standards incorporated by those responsible for developing the training initiative and required by the organization?
4. Does the evaluation structure provide a framework where emergent issues can be addressed? Can the design be modified to address participants' changing needs if the organization's strategic agenda changes without sacrificing objectives?
5. Can the design be carried out in the time allotted?
6. Does the design provide a mix of experiential learning exercises and other activities that appeal to diverse participants (i.e., different learning styles such as listening, discussing, and performing)?
7. Is the material logically and psychologically sequenced?
8. Is there appropriate redundancy in information and application practice presented in training?
9. Does the evaluation design allow for ongoing development of a learning climate?

Several possibilities exist for developing an evaluation system for training initiatives, and many designs can be combined to form other alternate designs. The question of which design to use depends on several factors. The nature of the training initiative and the practical considerations of the organization's work environment may dictate the appropriate design. The more complex the design, the more costly the evaluation effort. The availability of control groups and the ease of randomization are other factors that enter into the decision. The effects of factors outside the immediate environment must also be considered. If a design is less than optimum, the training staff must also be considered, and the training staff should be prepared to defend its action in terms of trade-offs. Additional information on evaluation designs can be found in other references (such as Emory & Cooper 1991).

CONCLUSION

This chapter presented basic information on training evaluation, including reasons why training doesn't occur, barriers to training, objectives and benefits of training, and common evaluation designs that can be useful in developing a reliable and valid evaluation scheme. The challenge for training personnel is to select an evaluation design that fits into the practical and economic framework of the organization.

In conclusion, today's training personnel must develop evaluations of their training efforts that consider a range of options given the available resources and overcome resource shortages and organizational constraints when they do occur. In any training effort, training personnel must work to document that training does have some beneficial effects in leadership's view. Effective training evaluation requires that training personnel pay attention to the following points:

1. Integrate the plan of training evaluation into the overall design of the training effort. Training evaluation should never be treated as a last minute "add on."

2. A training evaluation design (a) without pre- and posttraining measurements cannot measure behavior change and (b) without a control group cannot allow for valid evidence that any behavior change is due to the training. So both (a) and (b) are essential for significant evaluation of results.

3. Training personnel *must* work closely with employees, supervisors, managers, and executives on specific results to be expected at the end of training and the means of assessing those results.

4. A committee of various stakeholders should be responsible for evaluating *all* training initiatives.

5. To the extent practical, training evaluation should be conducted on as many levels as possible (i.e., Level 1 to Level 5).

6. Training evaluation should be related to on-the-job performance and directly tied to achievement of business results.

7. As noted earlier, organizational stakeholders must recognize that not all deficiencies can be corrected by training (e.g., selection, poor equipment, or ineffective management may be the problem) and should be willing to use training alternatives when and where appropriate.

8. Senior executives, managers and training personnel should not confuse attitudes with behavior (e.g., while they may want to train for proper attitudes toward delegation by supervisors or safety by employees, the real payoff is in changes in employees' *behavior*).

9. Training customers and training personnel should assess criteria for program participant selection and procedures. There is nothing to gain and little point in training the wrong people.

10. Training personnel should not be overlooked in the evaluation of training. This is a continuous rather than a one-time operation and extends to program content, outlines, nature of instruction, methods, training aids, facilities, and climate or atmosphere.

11. Where appropriate, outside resources should be used for a professional evaluation job (i.e., HRD consultants, statisticians, or educators).

In the end, the final success of training evaluation depends on the extent to which those who are responsible for evaluating training can overcome problems through a methodologically sound design and implementation scheme. The evaluation plan should be developed through selection of alternatives assessed against the objectives of the evaluation and existing constraints and resources. A familiarity with available resources, imposing constraints, and methodological alternatives will allow accurate, useful, and practical training effort evaluations. In addition, specific measures of the impact of training are important to the success of training evaluation, as is highlighted in Chapter 8.

CHAPTER 8

The When, What, and How of
Training Evaluation

As discussed in Chapter 7, training evaluation is of increasing importance to organizations as they continue to improve their competitive advantage. Training evaluation ensures that training initiatives are accountable and are meeting the needs of the organization in a cost-effective manner. Without evaluation, it is very difficult to show that training was the reason for any improvements in employee performance.

Many organizations recognize that training initiatives must be evaluated in order to ensure that employees are properly prepared for the future and possible skill obsolescence. For evaluations of training to be meaningful, organizations must be aware not only of the impact of particular training initiatives but must also focus attention on evaluating the extent to which the training function is aligned with the organization's strategic agenda.

This chapter takes a look at various forms of training evaluation. After introducing a model that focuses on designing training initiatives with an accompanying emphasis on training evaluation, the chapter will discuss the purpose and specific types of training evaluation criteria. Particular attention will be given to the when, what, and how of training evaluation. In addition, discussion will focus on collecting four types of data when evaluating training initiatives: measures of reaction, learning, behavior change, and organizational results. These criteria, based on Kirkpatrick's (1996) model, are widely used to evaluate organization training efforts. Further, discussion will emphasize the importance of ROI and cost–benefit analysis as evaluation tools.

Next, the chapter will discuss the importance of conducting a broader evaluation of the training function or system by highlighting the training audit. The chapter will end with a discussion of recent calls for improving training evaluation and briefly discuss the results-based and the balanced scorecard approaches to training evaluation.

THE ORGANIZATION AND DESIGN OF EVALUATIONS OF TRAINING INITIATIVES

The considerations for developing evaluations of training initiatives must include a formal diagnosis of an organization's strategic agenda, HRD and training needs, and the training efforts. This diagnosis should specify training evaluation objectives, evaluation criteria, and resources and constraints that will be encountered in planning and implementing the evaluation process. Wherever evaluation is called for, the training staff must ensure that objectives are established in terms of clear statements that provide some amount of measurability. Criteria are those specific measures that establish whether or not objectives are met. As discussed in Chapter 7, resources and constraints include not only money, personnel, equipment, time, and space, but also attitudes, norms, and values of the organization towards training. From the possible training evaluation techniques, specific techniques are selected that will most likely achieve initiative objectives within given constraints and existing resources. This is a "systems analysis" approach applied to developing a training evaluation plan. The result is an action plan indicating roughly the objectives and procedures evaluating training.

For training evaluations that involve multiple components, specification of evaluation procedures for later sessions will most likely initially be vague; these are developed in more detail by the organization's training staff as their time of implementation draws closer. The important point is that thought is given by the training staff as to how the training initiatives tie together to meet the overall objectives of the training. The pyramiding of objectives enables the training staff to test assumptions concerning the ability of procedures at lower levels to meet objectives at higher levels.

There is a need for more carefully designed training evaluations, and training personnel should be concerned with developing two major components of a training initiative. First, the training content or activities to be included in the initiative should be identified. Second, an outline or program for training evaluation should be developed. Simply put, the training evaluation plan is created by (1) defining the organization's training needs, (2) deciding what has to be evaluated, (3) developing the training initiative with objectives and criteria clearly laid out to enable evaluation, and (4) developing an evaluation plan based on the objectives, criteria, and activities of the training initiative. Figure 8.1 presents a model for designing training initiatives with an accompanying evaluation component. The left side of the model illustrates the *training design process* and presents the steps for developing the training initiative content. The right side of the model, labeled *evaluation design process*, presents steps necessary for designing the evaluation plan. Since the focus of this chapter is training evaluation, the right side of the model is of immediate concern.

Figure 8.1
Model for Designing Training Programs with Accompanying Evaluation Plans

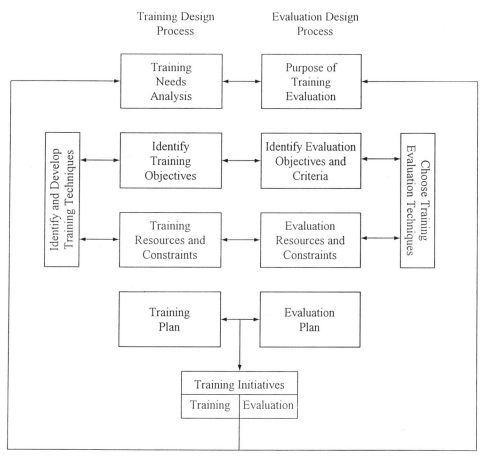

TRAINING EVALUATION PURPOSE AND CRITERIA

The first step in planning training evaluation is determining the purpose for evaluating the initiative: What do you want to know about the training initiative? Each kind of question necessitates consideration of how the evaluation initiative should be designed to provide answers. Stufflebeam and colleagues (1971) discuss three purposes for evaluation relevant to training evaluation. First, evaluation can be used to identify differences in behavior. Individuals or groups may be compared to other individuals or groups, to ideals or standards (as in performance appraisal), or with themselves at different moments in time (a time-series study). This is a *comparative* evaluation. Evaluation can also investigate causes of behavior. The variables within a training initiative responsible for changes within individuals or groups can be identified through experimental manipulation. This is *explanatory* evaluation. Finally, a *predictive* analysis can evaluate how well training performance data correlate with other variables such as changes in individual job performance and/or system performance. The purpose for training evaluation will impact each step in developing both the content and evaluation components of the training initiative.

In order to ensure that a training effort attains the objectives for which it was designed, training effectiveness must be measured by the organization's training and nontraining staff. Providing valid and reliable measures of the training concerns several issues: when to conduct evaluations, what to measure, and how to measure.

WHEN TO CONDUCT EVALUATIONS

The evaluation process actually begins before any employee receives training. By identifying areas for improvement, the needs analysis conducted prior to the design of training initiatives serves as the first stage of training evaluation, known as *formative evaluation*. Surveys or tests conducted to identify training needs can later serve as pretraining measures to evaluate how much learning took place. The design of learning objectives likewise should reflect the need to establish measurable, achievable criteria that can be used to evaluate the impact of the training initiative. The final part of a formative evaluation involves examining the initiative design to make sure it will have the desired impact.

In contrast to formative evaluation, a *summative evaluation* takes place after initial implementation of a training initiative. This evaluation looks at whether the training initiative is fulfilling its purpose and turning out employees who have achieved the desired training objectives. Besides evaluating the success or failure of a completed training effort, summative evaluations are useful for identifying ways to improve an ongoing training initiative.

The following sections look at each type of evaluation in greater detail.

Formative Evaluation

Formative evaluation measures the potential effect of a training initiative. Conducted during initiative design and development, a formative evaluation defines and refines training materials to maximize learning and achieve particular results. The purpose is to create a training initiative that has the greatest impact possible.

Ideally, the formative evaluation should involve people who have not participated in designing the initiative. This outside involvement allows the training initiative to be viewed in the same way that initiative participants will see it. Outside input can come from the following: one-to-one assessment, small group evaluation, and pilot testing. Each of these types of formative evaluation is discussed in more detail in the following sections.

One-to-One Evaluation

One-to-one evaluations involve a HRD, another training professional, and one person who is willing to participate in the learning process. Conducting several one-to-one evaluations are important to obtain a range of perspectives. The following types of people can provide the most assistance during this process: *subject matter experts* who make sure the content of the training initiative is technically correct; *HRD or other colleagues* who edit the initiative and comment on the positioning, set-up, or debriefing of activities or exercises; and *members of management and the target audience* who can review training techniques and materials for appropriateness, clarity of language, instructions, and effect.

A formative evaluation can be as simple as asking someone for a few minutes of help working through a link, or calling a subject matter expert to see if two steps can be lumped together or if they must be performed separately. Including individuals who will provide the most trustworthy feedback provides the most useful data for the one-to-one evaluation by identifying and addressing problems for the course to be ready for the prepilot test.

Prepilot Test

A prepilot test measures the training initiative's impact on multiple participants. This type of test is especially useful for group exercises or activities like games, simulations, and role plays. The test session gives the training personnel a chance to try out instructions and training techniques, and to assess group dynamics and synergy.

Ideally, members of the employee population who will participate in the training should be involved in the prepilot test. The prepilot test should be performed after problems identified during the one-to-one evaluations have been addressed, but training personnel should not wait to test the course until everything is perfect.

To conduct a prepilot test, the training initiative design should have progressed far enough that the training personnel have developed the following parts: materials needed to conduct training exercises and activities; written instructions for all activities and exercises, including guidelines for trainers and individual directions for different roles in group exercises; training objectives for the activities; and a checklist to track time, errors, omissions, mechanical problems, or logistic difficulties.

Using the information from the prepilot test checklist, trainers should get a picture of the type and degree of changes that need to be made for the initiative to operate smoothly. The training personnel should try to make all improvements identified through the prepilot test before conducting a final pilot test.

Pilot Test

The pilot test has many different names: alpha or beta test, field test, dry run, and pretest. Whatever the name, the purpose is the same: to obtain feedback from a large sample of the planned training audience. Properly conducted, the pilot test answers several questions about the training initiative's design. Does the initiative's content reflect the work environment? What improvements can be added? Has enough time been scheduled for each module or component? Does the initiative hold together? That is, do the transitions and themes work? And, are the practice items appropriate for the instructional content and job context?

In every way possible, the pilot test should resemble the actual training initiative. The only difference between the pilot test and the actual initiative is that an evaluator should hold feedback sessions with small focus groups of pilot test participants.

Pilot Test Evaluation

A pilot test evaluation is one of the most important parts of a formative evaluation. It is usually recommended that the person conducting the focus feedback sessions should be any member of the HRD function except the individuals, who will be busy running the course. The evaluator serves as both an impartial observer and a repository for participants' comments during the pilot test. At the end of the pilot test, evaluators record and report their own observations as well as conclusions offered by the test participants.

Training personnel should take note of the following items when observing the pilot test: the need for additional directions for activities; emotions and feelings shown by participants during activities or exercises; and participants' level of involvement during various parts of the initiative, including any point at which participants seem to tune out.

Besides getting specific information wanted by the training personnel, evaluators should ask the following questions when debriefing pilot test participants:

- How did the learning activities fulfill the module's objectives?
- Did the presentation and activities have a logical, coherent, and easy-to-follow sequence?
- Did each session cover a reasonable amount of information in the time available?
- Did presentations include enough well-chosen examples to clarify concepts?
- Did presentations use audiovisuals that clarified and supported the oral presentation?
- Did the learning methods stimulate adequate practice, activity, and thinking?
- Did ideas interrelate clearly and flow smoothly from one activity to another and from one module to another?

At the end of a lesson, could both the trainer and the participants identify what objectives had been achieved and where further explanation and practice were needed?

When evaluating trainers during the pilot test, a combination of methods gives the most comprehensive and useful evaluation. Trainer performance appraisals provide a manager's view of a trainer's performance and are the most common measurement criteria. Many organizations look at participants' evaluations of the trainer during the pilot test and posttraining trainee performance ratings to determine how many participants successfully transfer course material to their jobs. An increasingly popular method of evaluating trainers is peer review, in which other trainers complete their own questionnaires to identify a trainer's strengths and areas that need improvement.

At a minimum, three groups should receive a final report summarizing the findings of the pilot test evaluation. The first group is the training initiative's design and development team—the trainer, subject matter experts, and so on. This group will want minute details on how the participants and instructor(s) reacted to the training initiative. The second group needing evaluation results are the initiative trainers, who will want feedback on their work. Finally, customers (line managers and, more recently, senior leaders) of potential participants will want to know how the initiative was received. An evaluator may need to report the data differently for each group's evaluation report.

This written feedback marks the transition between formative evaluation and implementation of the actual training. It also begins the summative evaluation process since the evaluation forms used to pilot test participants can be revised to collect feedback throughout the training initiative's life span.

In order to ensure that a training effort attains the objectives for which it was designed, training effectiveness must be measured by the organization's training staff. Providing valid and reliable measures of the training concerns the what, when, and how of training evaluation.

What to Measure: Summative Evaluation

Summative evaluation assesses whether a new training initiative has met its objectives. It also helps to ensure the continued success of an ongoing training initiative. Summative evaluation measures the impact of training on participants and on the organization; it answers the question, "Did the initiative do what it was supposed to do so that the organization can meet its business goals?"

Ideally, the variables measured in training evaluation should incorporate the key features of the training effort as well as its expected results. In addition, the measurement of both the training effort and its outcome variables are necessary for in-progress and training-outcomes evaluation feedback. The training staff should avoid the tendency to measure only training-outcomes variables while neglecting training initiative variables altogether.

The successful implementation of training evaluations generally takes considerable time and learning. It must be empirically determined that training has been implemented appropriately; it cannot simply be assumed. In-process training evaluation feedback serves this purpose, guiding the implementation process and helping to interpret outcome data. Outcome measures are ambiguous without knowledge of how well the training initiative has been implemented. Measurement of the training initiative levels variables helps to determine the correct interpretation of outcome measures.

Points to cover in a summative evaluation of training include the following:

- *Tasks.* Are tasks sequenced properly for effective, efficient learning? Does the initiative include learning activities that are not boringly easy or overwhelmingly difficult?

- *Topics.* Does the initiative omit essential information? Is any information misleading or wrong?
- *Training methods.* Do participants feel they get enough feedback and practice? Do they and their supervisors consider the course useful? Do participants and trainers consider learning activities and materials to be worth the time and effort invested in them?
- *Tests.* Do tests demand that participants demonstrate—rather than describe—what they have learned? Do trainees consider the tests fair? Do participants and their supervisors consider the tests reasonable indicators of ability to perform on the job?
- *Productivity.* Has productivity—as measured by absenteeism, turnover, rework rates, or quality tests—improved for individuals or groups after training?

Summative evaluation takes place after training has ended. The evaluation techniques used should cause as little disruption as possible. For example, training personnel should hand out forms to trainees during the last session and allow time at the end of class for filling out the forms. Trainers should also complete an evaluation form once the initiative has concluded.

While trainers and participants can complete their feedback forms immediately after training, measuring the impact of training on performance will take longer. Supervisors observing trained employees' performance can provide some qualitative information about the effectiveness of training within a few weeks of an initiative's conclusion. Obtaining hard data—such as changes in absenteeism, output, errors, and so on—involves tracking specific criteria over longer periods of time.

HOW TO MEASURE

Measurement of training and its outcome variables involves operationalizing the variables so that appropriate data can be collected. This includes providing operational definitions of the variables that specify empirical information needed and how it will be collected. Operational definitions are extremely important in measurement because they provide precise guides about what characteristics of the training effort are to be observed and how they are to be observed. They tell training evaluators exactly how to measure training and outcome variables. For example, two key dimensions of good measures of surveys used in training evaluation are validity and reliability. *Validity* refers to whether a particular measure actually does measure what it purports to. *Reliability* refers to whether the measure is stable over time or situations (Nunnally 1978). Evaluation instruments that are valid and reliable can be used for training needs analysis, for guiding the implementation of training, and for evaluating the immediate and long-term training outcomes.

The criteria used in a training evaluation initiative will depend on its purposes. Whatever the purposes of the evaluation, training personnel can make use of five general categories, adapted from Suchman (1967):

1. Evaluation of *effort* assesses input, regardless of output. The questions "What did you do?" and "How well did you do it?" are addressed.

2. Evaluation of *performance* focuses on the results of the initiative. This requires clear statements of objectives; it asks "Did any change occur?" and "Were objectives achieved?"

3. Evaluation of *adequacy* determines how effective the initiative was. For example, participants in an initiative may exhibit considerable practical application change, but the number of participants may be inadequate in determining the benefits of the initiative for the organization.

4. Evaluation of *efficiency* is concerned with alternate ways of achieving the same ends that are more efficient in terms of time, money, human resources, materials, and convenience.

5. Evaluation of *process* focuses on the operation of a training initiative, with emphasis on how and why it works or does not work.

While several criteria have been tested through the years, at least four components proposed by Kirkpatrick almost forty years ago have been included in training evaluation: reaction to training, learning changes, transfer of training, and results (Kirkpatrick 1994). Performance Resources Organization has recently updated this framework to bring in the concept of ROI (Phillips 1996). Each one of these areas are discussed in more detail in the following sections.

Assessing Employee Reactions

Employee reactions to training are evaluated by conducting interviews or administering questionnaires to participants. Here, the training personnel are interested in whether participants liked the initiative, whether they thought the instruction was clear and helpful, and/or whether they believe that they learned the material. Measuring employee reaction from training is absolutely essential. Gaining direct feedback from a customer (that is, initiative participants) is important to measure satisfaction with the different parts of the initiative. In addition, this feedback provides needed input on the strengths and weaknesses of the training process, including issues such as initiative content, duration, handout materials, videos, experiential exercises, simulations, games, and even the learning climate. Phillips (1997) notes that this level of evaluation is important with new initiatives, for which initial feedback enables initiative sponsors to make adjustments.

Training personnel should include input on specific action items generated from the initiative when collecting data on participants' reactions. This can be accomplished through a series of questions which determine how participants plan to implement what they have learned, step by step. This action planning approach requires initiative participants to think about specific areas where the material can be applied and assists in the transfer of the learning to their work environment.

To effectively measure participants' reactions, training personnel should conduct surveys of trainees through the life span of the training initiative. Training personnel should compare survey results over time to detect shifts in participants' views of the initiative. These shifts may signal a need to update the content, replace the trainer, or make other adjustments to the initiative.

Training personnel should develop a standard series of questions for gathering participants' reactions. Standardizing these questions allows the tracing of participants' responses to an initiative across time. It also provides a way to compare one training initiative to another, or to a different type of intervention. While the exact number and types of questions to ask will depend on the course objectives, all feedback forms should ask trainees about the following points: demographics, activities, training materials, trainer qualifications, job relevance, initiative characteristics, and initiative objectives.

Initiative participants should complete evaluation forms before the final session ends. Data collected from the evaluation forms should be tabulated, analyzed, and reported on a regular basis using a schedule that reflects the type of initiative and its key initiative sponsors (i.e., line managers). For example, a training initiative for launching a new product or service will have a different reporting schedule than an established management training or development initiative.

The summary report should indicate how participants felt about the initiative. It should summarize participants' perceptions of the trainers, training media and materials, training methods, and training activities. No feedback report, however, can make conclusions about whether employees acquired the KSAOCs intended. That information comes only after the second level of evaluation: measuring learning or the amount of changes to KSAOCs.

While positive employee reactions are necessary for training to be successful, positive employee reactions do not necessarily mean that training will lead to changes in knowledge or performance (Alliger & Janak 1989). In fact, trainee reactions constitute the lowest level of training evaluation (Birnbauer 1987) and often can be misleading. Many studies have confirmed a lack of correlation between overall participant satisfaction and actual learning and subsequent application of the initiative material (Phillips 1997). While feedback is essential to judge satisfaction with initiative participants, it is ineffective as an overall evaluation of the initiative in terms of learning application and results. Level 1 reaction information can be useful for fine-tuning some aspects of the training initiative such as scheduling and mode of teaching; however, additional levels of evaluation are needed on learning changes, transfer of training, and results.

Assessing Employee Learning

For most training initiatives, participants are expected to learn something. Learning objectives usually focus on changes in KSAOCs. With increased emphasis on building learning organizations, the issue of measuring learning in training programs is especially important. Tests on the training material are commonly used for evaluating learning and can be given both before and after training to compare scores. Of course, learning enough to pass a test does not guarantee that the participant can *do* anything with what was learned. However, learning tests should be considered since they are objective, reliable, and easy-to-administer tools for evaluating training effectiveness.

Training evaluators can choose from several options for measuring whether participants have learned what they should have from the course. While objectives testing is important, organizations have devised a variety of measures to assess KSAOCs acquisition. Other methods include a variety of assessments, such as self-assessments, team assessments, facilitator assessment, performance testing, simulations, case studies, skill practices, role plays, and experiential learning exercises. Which option to use depends on the nature of the training and the types of KSAOCs the initiative was designed to instill. The discussion below outlines objective testing, simulation, and trainer observation options in more detail.

Objective Testing

Administering a test after training can help tell whether participants have learned relevant skills or knowledge. But unless employees took the same test before training, a good test score could simply reflect prior learning and not any benefit related to the initiative. An alternative is to compare trained employees' test scores to those of an untrained control group of employees, but few organizations are large enough to conduct this types of assessment. A good test score also does not guarantee transfer of learned knowledge and skills to the job. The greater the predictive validity of the test used, however, the more likely that transfer of training will take place for high scorers.

Simulations

As noted in Chapter 5, simulations evaluate a participant's ability to perform a specific task or a series of tasks, or to apply knowledge to a task. Simulations are best suited for training that involves equipment (such as computers) for discrete operations (such as parts assembly). For leadership training and development, simulations might involve in-basket or critical-incident exercises. Unlike objective testing, simulations measure application of knowledge to a task and more closely predict transfer of training to the job. Like tests, however, a high score on a simulation exercise does not necessarily reflect learning gained through training, unless pretesting or a control group is used.

Trainer Observations

Ideally, a trainer is a skilled observer of performance. Once training has ended, most trainers find it difficult to recall details about each person's performance. However, a trainer usually can provide feedback about the group as a whole. After completing a major portion of a training initiative, trainers should fill out a feedback sheet rating participants' mastery of the module's objectives and suggesting revisions that might improve the initiative. Helpful questions include the following:

- What learning activities, lecturettes, discussions, or other activities went well?
- What learning activities, lecturettes, discussions, or other activities need modification? How should they be modified?
- Did the module(s) move too quickly or too slowly for the trainer or the participants? Specify which module(s) had poor pacing.
- Did participants seem to find the information easy or difficult to understand? Specify the types of information where this happened.
- Did participants understand course notes, participant activities, and instructions? Specify the parts that participants seemed to find confusing.

Phillips (1997) suggests that a certain percentage of training initiatives should be targeted for learning measurement. Therefore, training personnel must develop specific criteria to select those initiatives by which learning will be measured. Measuring learning is critical when the organization has determined it is important for participants to have prescribed KSAOCs that are necessary and essential for job success. In situations where competency building, major change, and transformation are underway, high levels of learning assessment would be required. In areas where a large body of technical knowledge must be accumulated, as in knowledge of information technology, knowledge assessment becomes critical.

Although measuring participants' learning is important because it provides some assurance that participants possess the desired KSAOCs, there is still no assurance of application on the job. Consequently, Level 3 evaluation is needed to determine the specific application of KSAOCs.

Assessing Application or Transfer of Training

Perhaps the most critical issues of any training is the transfer of acquired KSAOCs to actual on-the-job application. Transfer of training or Level 3 evaluation concerns whether behavioral or performance changes taught in training are expressed on the job. Can participants now do things they could not before (e.g., negotiate or conduct an appraisal interview)? Do they demonstrate new behaviors on the job? Has their performance improved? A follow-up evaluation takes time, adds cost to the training process, and is often disruptive. And, according to Phillips (1997) these three issues alone have kept many organizations from appropriately using Level 3.

There are many ways transfer of acquired KSAOCs can be conducted. The most common ways to collect data for Level 3 are: follow-up surveys; follow-up questionnaires; observation on the job; interviews with participants and their coworkers, managers, and key customers; follow-up focus groups; initiative assignments; action planning; performance contracting; and initiative follow-up sessions. The challenge for training personnel is to select methods that fit the organization's culture, budget, and time constraints.

Positive transfer of training is perhaps the most critical goal of training. Since training represents a step toward improving job performance and/or organizational effectiveness, a lack of transfer in KSAOCs to the job may indicate a poor training effort.

A quality training initiative can ensure participants acquire and demonstrate certain KSAOCs within the initiative's controlled learning environment. But once participants leave this controlled setting, the training function alone cannot guarantee participants will apply their newly learned KSAOCs on the job. Transfer of learning is a partnership among the interested parties. Without this partnership, transfer of training becomes more difficult to track, and the odds of any transfer taking place drop.

Broad and Newstrom (1992) recommend devising strategies for transfer of training that can be implemented before, during, and after training. A few examples follow:

Before Training

• Plan the timing carefully, avoiding seasonal or cyclical busy times.

- Provide participants with pretraining assignments, such as readings or on-the-job problems, to bring to the training initiative.
- Review proposed training with supervisors; discuss the training objectives and how they will impact work.

During Training

- Send work units as a group rather than individuals.
- Provide a substitute on the job so the participant will not be "swamped" with accumulated work upon return.
- Simulate on-the-job conditions as much as possible.
- Ask trainees to visualize themselves applying their new KSAOCs.
- In small groups, discuss the pros and cons of using the new KSAOCs; develop an action plan.

After Training

- Debrief supervisor and/or coworkers.
- Schedule regular meetings to discuss progress and any remediation needed.
- Provide an information or support hotline.

Conditions that improve the likelihood that initiative participants will use their new KSAOCs on the job include the following.

Including Line (Senior) Management in Initiative Design

Training personnel should include line management in initiative design to make sure the equipment and techniques taught mirror the way employees perform tasks in the actual job. For ongoing training initiatives, training personnel need to maintain contact with managers to keep up with new job tasks that should be incorporated into the course.

Ensure Supervisor Support for Employee Development

Line managers should actively participate in assessing employee needs prior to training, in providing opportunities for employees to use their new KSAOCs during and after training, and in rewarding trained employees for using their learning on the job. Additionally, line managers should spend time debriefing the training with participants once they return to the job.

Organizational Climate That Promotes Training

An organizational climate supportive of employee development is necessary for training initiatives to have a real impact. Organizational climate and policies should promote training as being important to achieving organizational results and success. Work and production schedules should build in time for employees to attend training. Organizational reward initiatives should recognize participants' achievements and the managers who support employee development.

Well-Planned (Just-In-Time or Real-Time) Training Schedules

If training is delivered shortly before or after a person receives a major increase in job responsibilities or a promotion, its relevance increases and the trainee is more likely to use the new skills. Otherwise, it is best to deliver training during periods when an individual's work routine is stable and predictable so the trainee will have as much pressure-free time to practice new ideas and behaviors.

For many training initiatives, a check of KSAOC application is sufficient for the evaluation process. For others, however, a connection with actual business performance is desired, since it is possible to obtain positive application of knowledge and skills, yet have no impact on an organization performance measure. For example, if the needs analysis is inadequate or improper, KSAOCs acquired in the initiative will not necessarily improve the desired organization performance measures. When evidence of an impact on organizational objectives is needed, the next level of evaluation is necessary to determine performance improvement.

Assessing Results or Bottom-Line Measures

Transfer of training to the job should produce measurable improvement in the trained employee's performance, as well as the supervisor's evaluation of the employee. The ultimate goal of improving job performance is to contribute to the organization's bottom line. Organizational leaders (and training personnel) are interested in finding answers to questions such as, "Did the organization actually save money following the training initiative?" or "How well were the training dollars invested?"

As discussed earlier, today's leaders are interested in knowing how training actually improved the business in terms that they really understand. Leaders now require bottom line performance from major training initiatives. The difficulty in making this connection stems from the origin of most training efforts. Sometimes it is difficult to understand the relationship between organization problems, challenges, and opportunities and a specific training need. Some needs analysis processes do not link KSAOC deficiencies to organization performance problems or opportunities. Thus, a more complete needs analysis process may be needed to include measures of organization results. When this is the case, it is possible to link training efforts to their impact on organization results. Particularly in tight budgetary times, the training function must show senior leadership how employee development efforts affect overall productivity and profits. Results are evaluated by measuring the effect of training on the achievement of organizational objectives. For example, recognizing there are many factors that can influence a particular organization performance measure in an organization, the training evaluation strategy also must include a method to isolate the effects of the training initiative from other influences. A variety of methods are available to accomplish this task: use of a control group arrangement, trend line analysis of performance data, use of forecasting methods of performance data, participants' estimate of training's impact (percentage), supervisor's estimate of training's impact (percent), management estimate of training's impact (percentage), use of previous studies, direct reports of other factors, calculating or estimating the impact of other factors, and use of customer impact.

This step often is overlooked in training evaluation, largely because many training personnel believe the analysis would prove overwhelming. But much of the data used to evaluate the organizational impact of training already is compiled regularly for department reports and other purposes. All training personnel have to do is analyze this data for before- and after-training effects. Sources of information to examine for posttraining effects include the following.

Productivity Reports

Look at hard production data, such as production turnover, sales reports, task completion times, error rates, or manufacturing totals. Comparing figures before and after training can help leaders and training personnel determine whether any training-related performance improvements have taken place that affect the organization's bottom line.

HR Reports

Information gathered for HR purposes may show training outcomes that affect organizational goals. Safety reports, for example, may show reductions in workplace accidents or equipment damage after employees received training. Training personnel should also examine other records for reductions in absenteeism, grievance filings, turnover, customer complaints, and so on.

Cost Analysis

Training personnel should use the costs of trainers' fees, materials, facilities, travel, training time, and the number of trainees to determine the hourly cost of training for each participant.

The specific sources of data and approaches to measuring organization impact vary. Monitoring organization performance is the most common and credible approach (Phillips 1997). Specific performance measures are monitored for improvement after an initiative is conducted. Other techniques that have proven useful in recent years to measure impact include action planning, performance contracts, and the use of follow-up questionnaires.

It is critical for leaders and training personnel to define specific criteria to determine which initiatives should be evaluated at Level 4. Criteria include such items as the importance of the training initiative in meeting organizational goals, the size of the target audience, and the cost of the initiative.

Though the Level 4 results or bottom-line evaluation is extremely important and pushes training evaluation to the next level desired in many organizations, it still falls short of what is considered to be an ideal evaluation. It is possible for a training initiative to have a positive impact on the bottom line or important business results, yet represent a negative ROI. In this situation, the cost of the training initiative has exceeded monetary benefits. Because of this situation, the ultimate level—the ROI—must be calculated for some select training efforts.

Measuring and Calculating ROI

ROI has been used to evaluate performance of business endeavors for many years. The purchase of equipment, acquisition of another company, or the development of a new product line or service are subjected to a ROI methodology, in which the payoff of the investment is captured. Today, more organizations are demanding the same evaluation of training for major training expenditures. The process requires two additional steps: The Level 4 organization results must be converted to monetary benefits, and the actual cost of the initiative must be captured.

Converting organization measures to monetary values is a very difficult task for some measures, such as market share and customer satisfaction. Fortunately, several techniques are available to make this conversion with reasonable accuracy. The process is applied methodically with the credibility and accuracy desired by many organizations: converting output to contribution, converting the cost of quality and employees' time, using historical costs, using internal and external experts, using data from external databases, and using participants', supervisors', senior leaders', and staff estimates.

When conducting an ROI impact, training initiative costs should include all direct and indirect costs. Typical training initiative costs leaders and training personnel should include development costs, initiative materials, trainer costs, facilities costs, travel/lodging/meals, participant salaries and benefits, and administrative–overhead costs.

Training personnel can select from a number of different methods for determining training's ROI. A traditional ROI formula involves the following steps:

Calculate the training return. The training evaluation should have produced some payoff measure, such as increased sales, the value of higher productivity, the costs savings of less equipment damage, and so on.

Figure the training investment. This figure reflects the total costs of conducting training.

Add together the following expenses:

Initiative expenses. Include expenses for participants and training personnel for travel, lodging, and food, as well as the salaries for trainers and facility rental.

Materials and equipment expenses. Factor in costs for materials, supplies, and equipment operations.

To figure total training investment, deduct from total expenses any offsetting factors:

Initiative revenues. Paybacks from training might come from program participants' accumulation of frequent flyer coupons, or from resale or rental of training materials.

Equipment revenues. Resale, rental, or reuse of training equipment for other purposes can offset the cost of purchasing the devices.

Subtract the training investment from the training return. This calculation yields net (after expenses) training return.

Calculate ROI by dividing the net training return by the training investment. This final calculation should yield a figure greater than one. If not, the organization has actually lost money by training employees.

In short, the ROI formula is the net program benefit as assessed in the analysis of changes in critical financial indices, divided by the program cost. A simple way of expressing this formula is

$$\text{ROI (percentage)} = \frac{\text{Benefits} - \text{Costs}}{\text{Costs}} \times 100$$

In reality, only a small number of training initiatives should receive Level 5 evaluation (Phillips 1997). Because of this, the criteria needed to select the initiatives are extremely important. Training personnel must ensure that the criteria and the initiatives identified for evaluation at this level are developed and ultimately approved by senior management. The importance of senior leadership involvement at this level cannot be underestimated since training initiatives selected for evaluation at this level are critical to the organization's success, represent major investments, involve large audiences, or have high visibility in the organization or to external customers.

As mentioned previously, the levels of evaluation described above should be viewed, not as an individual approach, but as a cascading process of increased sophistication. Each level provides useful and important information. An overall process that makes use of techniques from each level is more likely to generate useful data that verifies the impact of training on the organization and its members.

Benchmarking

To conduct a thorough evaluation of a training initiative, training functions can benchmark their practices against the best in the industry (Ford 1993). Benchmarking is a logical process involving systematic steps or phases. When implemented successfully, the benchmarking process should be an integral part of an organization's evaluation of training. Benchmarking training analyzes critical areas for improvement and is based on collecting data from organizations that have been identified as having the best practices in training. This ultimately leads to action necessary to make improvements to move toward using the best practices in training. Benchmarking training provides the organization with information on key variables that are important to measuring and improving training.

A cost–benefit analysis approach can also be employed in evaluating training efforts.

Cost–Benefit Analysis

The ultimate evaluation questions on training initiatives evolve around utility. More specifically, is the gain to the organization in increased performance greater than the cost of the training enough to justify the investment? Answering this question requires that dollar values be placed on various levels of performance, productivity, and results, and that various training costs be computed. Because of its focus on utility, cost–benefit analysis (CBA) is a natural choice of evaluation methodology for leaders and training personnel who are consistently confronted with a bottom-line approach to making decisions around investments in training initiatives.

While demonstrating the costs and benefits associated with training initiatives may be difficult, it is important for showing top management the value of training for the organization. For example, in one case the net return for a training initiative for bank supervisors was calculated to be $148,000 over a five-year period. At Ford, all training programs are evaluated against the criterion of product line profitability. A tracking system shows costs and revenue for training facilities and individual courses (Mathieu & Leonard 1987; Bernardin & Russell 1998).

CBA presents information on economic efficiency. The most common application of CBA is to decide which of a set of alternative projects are economically feasible, and which of those is most satisfactory should only one be affordable (Mishan 1976; Hawthorne 1987; Bernardin & Russell 1998). Thus, a preview of a training initiative can be afforded by CBA. In addition, CBA methodology can be employed in retrospective analyses that examine which completed course or training initiative was most successful in terms of cost–benefit criteria. Retrospective CBA is more straightforward to accomplish than prospective analysis because it depends on training initiative-generated data in places where prospective analysis relies on economic theory, projections, and assumptions. Retrospective CBA, however, may also use economic theory and similar assumptions.

Costs

As the role of training has increased in organizations, it has also become big business. For organizational leaders and training personnel, even more compelling evidence of training costs comes from the budget allocated to training initiatives. As highlighted in the discussion on ROI, training costs are fairly easy to compute. They consist of nonrecurring and recurring expenses. Nonrecurring costs are those associated with the development of training initiatives (such as materials used by the developer and his or her salary), while recurring costs are those associated with conducting such initiatives. Recurring costs can be further broken down into those that are fixed (such as facilities) and those that are variable (such as handouts provided to initiative participants and participants' salaries while they are off the job).

Traditionally, the substantial budget costs of training often lead organizations to see only the cost per trainee and consider cutting training initiatives to save costs. Though it may often be appropriate to cut ineffective training initiatives, it is impossible to judge effectiveness by costs alone. Often, such shortsighted decision making may cost more in lost productivity than it saves in initiative expenses. CBA requires that organizational managers and training personnel pay attention to the benefits of training.

Benefits

While training costs are fairly easy to conceptualize and compute, the same is not true of the gains or benefits from training. The estimation of gains requires that evaluators not only place a dollar value on various levels of performance, but also take into account several factors that can affect these dollar values (e.g., the diminishing effect of training over time and turnover rate among those who have been trained). The estimation of the dollar payback associated with program participants' performance after receiving training provides valuable information to the organization. Since the results of the experimental design will indicate any differences in behavior between those trained versus those untrained, the training personnel can then estimate for that particular group of employees (e.g., leaders or engineers) what this difference is worth in terms of the salaries of those employees. Another factor that should be considered when estimating the benefit of training is the duration of the training's impact; that is, the length of time during which the improved performance will be maintained. While probably no initiatives will show benefits forever, those that incur longer-term improved performance will have greater value to the organization. While major conceptual and methodological advances in the measurement of training benefits have been made in recent years, actual applications are still few.

Recent research indicates that organizations with sophisticated training systems look to training to support corporate strategy and change much more often than they look for measuring financial returns on training investment. At successful companies, such as ICI, Royal Mail's Anglia Division, Yamazaki Machinery UK, and Frizzell Financial Services, the organizations focused on *pay-forward*, a term used to describe the benefits from training in terms of the company's capacity to learn and change. This differs from *pay-back*, which refers to straight financial returns from the training (Lee 1996).

An excellent example of training evaluation in practice is the experience of American Express Travel Related Services (TRS) continuous improvement efforts. Evaluation is embedded througout their Global Sales Learning System, where they measure how satisfied participants are, how well they are acquiring skills during training, how well they apply the skills on the job, and the resulting business outcome. They also measure satisfaction of key stakeholders in terms of their responsiveness (timely delivery of learning); relevance (learning driven by and focused on business needs); economics (learning delivered at the right price); effectiveness (sustained knowledge–skill transfer and impact); and efficiency (especially reduced rework and redundancy).

Just more than a year into the design and development of their Global Learning System, those responsible for the training effort were able to report the following facts to senior leadership:

1. Ninety-five percent of participants in all sales learning rated the training "excellent."

2. Sales training costs had been reduced by 40 percent through the elimination of unnecessary and redundant course offerings.

3. Applying negotiating for profitability skills, the Corporate Services group renegotiated 220 accounts with airline industry customers (who had called on TRS to restructure commission) in just thirty days. TRS secured new contracts with 90 percent of these "at risk" accounts, profitably retaining millions of dollars in ongoing business.

In spite of various tools and inventories available for evaluating training, Shandler notes, "The process of training evaluation, while improving, still has a long way to go" (1996, 107). The greatest emphasis (84%) is placed on measuring participants' reactions to courses, and the least emphasis (43%) is placed on measuring changes in business results attributable to training.

Shandler suggests that we need to go beyond the use of traditional evaluation mechanisms to start the process of reengineering the training function to align it with what he refers to as the "new corporate agenda." Shandler, like others (Buckley & Caple 1984; Bramley & Hullah 1987) suggest the use of a comprehensive and strategic training audit to evaluate the training function. The next section discusses the training audit in more detail.

TRAINING AUDIT

The concept of the training audit (TA) as a vehicle for evaluating training initiatives has been recently introduced by several authors (Buckley & Caple 1984; Bramley & Hullah 1987). A TA is usually for senior management when they are seeking to review the activities (training initiatives) of the training function. Shandler (1996) suggests that a bold and comprehensive TA, one that looks at not only training practices and HRD practices is needed to evaluate training. Unlike those who have previously recommended the use of a TA, Shandler is concerned with strategic training audits which can provide a "big picture" view of "how you are doing."

According to Bramley and Hullah (1987), there are two major aspects to auditing training: (1) auditing the training system in order to discover how professional it is and to what extent it contributes to the well-being of the organization, and (2) auditing a specific training initiative to discover how well run it is and also how well it fits into the organizational context.

Auditing a training initiative has four stages: familiarization; examining the preactivity preparation; auditing the training initiative itself, and examining the postinitiative learner support.

Stage One: Familiarization

The intent in the familiarization stage is to take a thorough look at what the training initiative is supposed to be doing, where it has come from, and why it is there. It is also necessary to discover if there is any evidence that the training initiative is actually of value to the organization. Some of the key areas and questions that need to be asked are as follows:

1. *Aims, intentions, and objectives*
   - What changes are expected to result from this initiative in terms of individual performance levels? Organizational effectiveness?
   - How do these changes relate to overall corporate objectives?
   - Whose objectives are controlling the initiative—the organization (i.e., training committee function or HR manager); the participants (i.e., fine tuning of initiative objectives or training HRD personnel)?

2. *Needs analysis*
   - How was the needs analysis done? When? By whom? By what methods?
   - How wide was the consultation on needs?
   - Where is the emphasis on needs? Individual? Organizational? Remedial–Developmental?

3. *Target population/demand*
   - How are people selected for this training? Line manager–appraisal system? Self-nomination? HR function? HRD function?
   - On what basis is the selection made?
   - To what extent are participants ready for the initiative and the standards implicit in the training objectives?
   - What, if any, procedures are used to integrate nominations with the overall HRD planning system?

4. *Evaluation*
   - Is a report on the training initiative available?
   - Has a previous audit been undertaken? What were the recommendations?
   - What evaluative and implementation feedback data about this initiative are held by the training function?
   - What is the cost of the initiative?
   - What evidence is there of benefits?

According to Bramley and Hullah (1987), this stage could sometimes be the complete audit. If the activity is not linked to organizational requirements and does not appear to be meeting a need, the audit could be stopped at the end of this stage.

An important aspect of the familiarization stage is that it ought to be possible to find some links between the training initiative or activity and the organization's objectives. A simple case is as follows: Sales trainers have objectives of trying to impart new product knowledge and the techniques for using it in selling; sales personnel attending the training will have objectives of learning something that will help them to get orders for the new products; sales managers will have the objectives of reaching targets and obtaining new sales; and the organization will have the intention of obtaining sales volume that matches the potential product volume and that will maintain or increase their share of the market.

Collecting information about this chain of intentions can only be done by visiting and listening to supervisors and managers along the chain, in the areas where they work. This is standard procedure for external trainer consultants, but it is often neglected by internal HRD personnel.

Stage Two: Preinitiative Preparation

It is important to determine the extent to which individuals attending a training initiative know why they are attending. If they are not aware of their reason for attending, then the first part of the training initiative is an uphill battle to establish objectives for these individuals that will commit them to learning something and thus underpin motivation.

The training policy document should lay down the clear responsibilities and roles for supervisors and leaders as well as HRD personnel. If the "right" people are not being selected, and if the purpose of their attending training is not clarified, there is little likelihood of the training resulting in improved performance. The questions that might be asked in this part of the TA are: (1) What form does the preinitiative briefing take? Who does the briefing? Are learning objectives clarified and agreed? What is the extent of trainer involvement?; (2) How are the training objectives communicated? Do the supervisors and line managers understand them?; (3) What is the individual expected to do differently at the end of the initiative?; (4) How long before the initiative did the briefing take place?; (5) Was any preinitiative preparation necessary? Activity? Reading? Other?; and (6) Was it carried out?

Stage Three: Auditing the Training Initiative

A good place to start the examination of the training initiative in a TA is by looking at which objectives are actually controlling the learning. During the familiarization phase of the TA, the auditor will have discovered what the objectives are; the emphasis now changes to the way in which they are being used.

The questions that might be asked at this point in the TA are

1. *Training initiative objectives*
   - Have the training staff openly discussed and agreed upon the objectives?
   - Are the objectives clear and unambiguous?
   - Does the achievement of the objectives mean complete achievement of the training need, or is some on-the-job training required?

- To what extent are training personnel familiar with the participants' own learning objectives? How different or similar are the participant's own learning objectives to the actual program learning objectives?

2. *Training initiative structure*

   - On what principles is the training initiative structured?
   - Is there a satisfactory balance between practice reflection and theory input?
   - How satisfactory is the duration of the training initiative and the length of the working day?
   - Does the balance of the training initiative reflect the different degrees of importance attached to the objectives?

3. *Training methods and media*

   - On what basis have the training methods been chosen?
   - Are optimal training methods being used, given the characteristics of the learners?
   - Do training methods and media provide variety and encourage learning?
   - What is the quality and readability of handouts and other training aids?
   - Was the criteria used to select the training method or combination of methods clear?

4. *Evaluation–Feedback*

   - What form of assessment of progress is being used during the training initiative?
   - Is each assessment method reliable and timely?
   - Where practical or written tests are being used: Are the test items appropriate? Are there sufficient test items? Have the tests been piloted? How reliable is the marking guide?
   - Is debriefing incorporated at appropriate places throughout the training effort?
   - How is feedback given to the participants?
   - How is feedback used by the trainers?
   - Are guidelines for providing feedback used by participants and trainers?
   - Is there sufficient flexibility to allow remedial work?
   - Are summarizing and consolidating sessions built into the training initiative?
   - Are training initiative evaluation reports written? To whom are they sent? Is any action taken as a result of these reports?

Stage Four: Posttraining Initiative Learner Support

The learning model that underlies most training is: (1) the individual wants to improve; (2) learning through training; (3) changes in individuals' KSAOCs and attitudes; (4) changes in individuals' work performance; and (5) changes in organizational effectiveness. The focus is on the individual, and the process is one of encouraging her or him to learn something said to be useful, and then expecting them to find uses for the learning. The transfer of learning needs to be supported by an action plan, a suitable organizational climate and, usually, a sympathetic line manager. The training auditor(s) should investigate the extent to which posttraining initiative learner support is given. The kinds of questions that should be asked during the investigation of the posttraining initiative learning support are the following:

1. *Posttraining initiative debriefing*
   - What form does the posttraining initiative briefing take?
   - Who does it?
   - Are action plans reviewed and priorities set?
2. *Constraints*
   - What constraints, if any, have been placed on the employee's ability to put into effect what they have learned?
   - What level of support is being given to the achievement of action plans developed during the training?
3. *Performance levels*
   - Is there a gap between the levels achieved during training and competent job performance back in the actual work setting?
   - Is support available to close this gap? If so, what kind and who monitors the process?
4. *Evaluation*
   - What changes have been achieved in terms of different individual performance levels? Increased levels of organizational effectiveness?
   - What criteria of effectiveness are being used?
   - Who is responsible for assessing changes?
   - How do the changes achieved relate to those planned (and discovered by the auditor during the familiarization stage)?
   - What objectives have been achieved in terms of organizational objectives? Individual learning objectives? Additional HRD personnel objectives?

In conclusion, the TA must concern itself first with the fit between the training function overall, the training initiatives it undertakes on behalf of the organization, and the organization's strategic agenda. This can only be done in discussions with top-, middle-, and lower-level leaders. Training personnel must understand that conducting strategic training audits as suggested by Shandler (1996) will contribute to the reinvention and ongoing learning needed in the training function in order to ensure that training helps the organization drive improved performance, change, and transformation.

In concluding the discussion on training evaluation, it is important to take a look at recent calls for improving training evaluation and corresponding suggestions for improving training evaluation.

CALLS FOR IMPROVING TRAINING EVALUATION

In response to calls for more accountability and training effectiveness, several authors have criticized traditional efforts to evaluate training and suggested alternative techniques. For example, Murphy (1997) believes that the approach employed by training (management) professionals over the years has proven to be a dismal failure and is opposite of the type of training actually required. Murphy suggests that trainers should first concentrate on improving performance and business results and should recognize the interaction between performance and development. He believes a "results" first approach is contrary to traditional training, which has been aimed at the supposed antecedents of results, including organizational culture, management competencies, knowledge, behavior, and attitudes.

Murphy also suggests that training that works (and can be easily evaluated) is training that taps the individual's accountability for near-term results. By focusing on their customer's urgent or immediate results every time they design a training effort, training professionals are able to clearly demonstrate the cause-and-effect relationship between training (learning) and results. In demonstrating a cause-and-effect relationship training professionals are able to answer the following question: What is the payoff of our training?

Like Murphy, Phillips (1996) recommends the use of a results-based human resource approach to evaluation which can be easily applied to training evaluation. The model places emphasis on achieving results and involves nine steps necessary to fully analyze, develop, and implement HR (training) programs. The steps are (1) needs analysis, (2) measurement and evaluation system, (3) program objectives, (4) program development, (5) program implementation, (6) cost monitoring, (7) data collection and analysis, (8) interpretation and conclusion, and (9) communicating results.

According to Phillips, steps number three, four, and five make up the traditional model where objectives are established and the program is developed and implemented. The other steps, which have received more emphasis in recent years, are necessary to place the proper emphasis on measuring the contribution of the new program, and thus prevent unneeded programs from being implemented.

Willyerd (1997) recently noted that much of the training in which our organizations invest is geared toward future performance, since after all, training is often an investment in long-term performance of people. However, measurement of training results have occurred with financial tools that look backward and are misleading. She suggests that we need to use performance indicators that look to the future. More specifically, Willyerd believes some different performance-measurement tools that have been proposed for general business use may provide a more balanced approach to training evaluation. In addition, she notes that these tools will ensure that a training or performance solution is strategically aligned, objectively evaluated, and quantitatively measured for results.

Willyerd recommends using the balance scorecard (Kaplan & Norton 1992), which tracks the key elements of a company's strategy using both financial and operational measures (i.e., drivers of future financial performance), as a tool for improving the effectiveness of training evaluation. Like Kirkpatrick's (1994) model, the balanced scorecard looks at four key areas of performance by providing answers to four basic questions:

1. How do we look to our shareholders? (Financial perspective)
2. How do customers see us? (Customer perspective)
3. What must we excel at? (Internal perspective)
4. Can we continue to improve and create value? (Innovation and learning perspective).

The balanced scorecard is intended to help ensure that all the critical performance measures are evaluated. It provides a check and balance so that one area is not overemphasized at the expense of another.

The use of the balance scorecard can be effectively applied to any training initiative or performance solution by training professionals. To ensure the initiative is strategically aligned with their customer's business objectives, training professionals must collect the department's vision and mission statements. If the customer does not have one, the training professionals should offer to assist in developing one, explaining that it will help them ensure that their product fully aligns with the department's business objectives. Training personnel should ask for any information on strategic initiatives that are in place. In addition to asking for performance standards during their front-end analysis, training personnel should also ask for critical success factors and measures from all four areas (financial, customer, internal, and innovation and learning perspectives). Performance measurements tied to the customer perspective might be percentage of repeat customers, percentage of complaints, number of new accounts, and so on.

Training personnel can also combine the balanced scorecard with a performance-measurement index tool, also called an objectives matrix. It enables training personnel and their customers to create a sort of Dow Jones industrial average for measuring performance. Furthermore, it is a performance-tracking tool for customers that they maintain themselves. Combining these tools will help training personnel track strategically aligned results in a quantifiable fashion, thus better addressing the question of, What results occurred because of the training?

As calls for increased accountability in training continue, and those in the training profession remain open to calls for improving training evaluation, we will find better and more effective ways to evaluate training. In improving the training evaluation process, we will be better able to show the training, HRD, and HR contribution to achievement of individual and organizational learning and the organization's strategic agenda.

CONCLUSION

Clearly, training customers want results. And evaluation is critical to demonstrating to customers that their investment in training has paid off. The last two chapters have emphasized the importance of viewing evaluation as key to the success of any training. This chapter has discussed a number of issues integral to training evaluation. In particular, the chapter highlighted the importance of when to conduct evaluations, how to conduct evaluations, and what to measure during evaluations. Organizations must begin their commitment to the evaluation process once a needs analysis is completed. The methods of evaluation should be selected during the step of designing the entire training intervention. In other words, evaluation is a front-end activity and an ongoing ritual.

In conclusion, it is important to remember that, while ideally training personnel should always undertake a comprehensive evaluation effort, at a minimum they need to do some kind of evaluation even if it is only on the reaction level. Regardless of whether evaluation is completed at the lowest (reaction) or highest level (strategic training audit), it must be a planned activity from the beginning of the initiative, or one cannot hope to demonstrate the value of training to one's customers.

CHAPTER 9

A Look to the Future of Training and Development

Peter Senge popularized the concept of *learning organization* in his book *The Fifth Discipline*. He described them as places "where people continually expand their capacity to create the results they truly desire, where new and expansive patterns of thinking are nutured, where collective aspiration is set free, and where people are continually learning how to learn together" (1990b, 3).

Learning organizations appear to be proficient in a number of activities: systematic problem solving, experimentation with new approaches, learning from their own experience and history, learning from the experiences and best practices of others, and transferring knowledge quickly and efficiently throughout the organization (Garvin 1993). Learning in firms such as General Electric, Pittsburgh Plate Glass (PPG), and Xerox has been traced using a learning perspective that involves three stages: (1) cognitive—members are exposed to new ideas, expand their knowledge, and begin to think differently; (2) behavioral—employees begin to alter their behavior; and (3) improvement of performance—changes in behavior lead to measurable improvement in results (Howard 1992).

In an organization dedicated to creating a learning environment, training is a top priority. Learning organizations do not simply appear. They are fostered by devoting time, energy, and resources on a continuous basis to the training and development of employees. Taking steps to encourage learning through training and development activities and forums is essential to improved understanding, performance, and effectiveness.

To help their organizations learn requires the training function to shed its current roles and adapt to the organization environment of the future. The training function must (1) adapt a more strategic role in the organization; (2) deal with the demands of training and developing the more diverse, knowledgeable workforce of the future; and (3) adapt and prove its value to the future of the organization.

The purpose of this final chapter is to offer a concluding look at the future of training by discussing the issues above and other related issues that will continue to shape what organizations will expect of their training professionals as we move into the next millennium. The chapter will also discuss a number of ways in which trainers might respond to the issues in the coming years. The chapter concludes with a discussion of a process for building training's strategic value.

THE EVER-CHANGING ROLE OF TRAINING

As the pace and complexity of change in organizations continues, training must become more closely integrated with the organization's strategic agenda. To do this, training staff will need a much wider exposure to the organization's internal and external environment. They will have to build more bridges with customers, both those in line units and those outside the organization.

Training professionals will have to help foster an environment for excellence by taking a proactive stance in linking training to organizational values and identifying strategic issues. This will require increased research on the impact of organization vision and strategy on HR and HRD, and an increased willingness to participate in strategy formulation and implementation.

The training function will also need to integrate itself more closely with a wide range of HR functions, such as recruitment, staffing, labor relations, employee relations, and organizational analysis. This may present problems for some staff who have spent years differentiating themselves from the "human resources," but today's employees want one-stop HR services that are organized to serve core processes. Further distancing of the training function from the rest of the organization, while arguably useful in the days when it could be swallowed by the rest of HR, will only antagonize customers in the future.

Indeed, the training function needs to take a strategic orientation from service provider to performance consultant, policy setter, and value purveyor. For example, in response to efforts to decentralize HR and their HRD efforts, some organizations have begun to push centralized HR and HRD functions into line units. Where this occurs, the training function of the future must be prepared for the fact that they may do very little training delivery. Rather, it may facilitate and support the creation of the training vision, strategy, and core values and then support line units in aligning themselves with all three. A related role for the training function will be to foster the development of individual, team, and organizational learning not by teaching but by helping people find ways to build learning strategies into their work.

Many training functions are still taking a "reactive" or "training" approach to their charge. Such approaches cast the training function as one focused on processing training requests and providing classroom training. This is how the training function grew and how they became successful.

Yet, these approaches do not serve the future training and development needs of organizations as well as they served the past, and failure to move beyond them will be taking a dangerous risk. There is no doubt that over the long term, reactive and classroom training services will be heavily automated, performed by line units and/or done by subcontractors to a much greater degree, leaving central training functions without a substantial business to be in.

By comparison, organizations will increasingly demand a "strategic," "customer," "performance improvement," and "accountability" orientation, in which they look to training to help solve problems, lead change, and foster a learning environment. These goals call for more work and performance analysis, organization development, visioning, and performance consulting services. Training professionals can add real value to their organizations by meeting such needs.

Most training functions have realized that they have been operating in some degree in a reactive posture. This is not atypical given that their past success and future demands are at cross purposes. But to continue to try to do the same will also be to take a large risk since the KSAOCs, products, and services required for a reinvented, new, and proactive training orientation are so different.

CHANGING TECHNOLOGY AND TRAINING PRODUCTS AND SERVICES

While hardware will capture a lot of headlines, the action will be in applications, not infrastructure, in knowledge workers and not their machines. The information content of jobs has already been increasing in recent years (Zuboff 1988). A great deal of work in organizations is already information and knowledge intensive, and it will become more so. This will lead to more specialized types of job duties and a need for higher-level critical thinking skills. In the American workforce as a whole, only 4 percent of new jobs in the year 2000 will require language, reasoning, and math skills at the lowest skill levels (Johnson & Packer 1987). Lower-skill jobs will increasingly disappear, be automated, or be outsourced.

Changes in technology, like other changes impacting training, will require that the training function offer a wider array of products and services for a broader array of customers. For example, only a few years ago, training functions were viewed as responsive when they offered introductory word processing, spreadsheet, and database courses. Now they must offer intermediate and advanced courses in these areas, as well as courses on the Internet, desktop publishing, programming, electronic mail, and statistical analyses. This pattern of increasing depth in specific technical and professional areas will continue because the rapid growth of specialized knowledge continues. An increasing focus on teams will add demands for both team skills and for cross-training of team members. In short, the audience for particular professional training is likely to expand, as organizations reduce the number of employees in some of those professions.

Other changes in such areas as process reengineering, quality management, strategic planning, performance measurement, organizational culture change, and customer service will add another set of demands for training and performance consulting. Customers will increasingly seek help for intact work groups and even entire organizations, more often on-the-job and on a just-in-time basis rather than as mass training before it is really needed.

As the boundaries of organizations and the functional units within them continue to blur, new training audiences will come into focus. Training staff will be called upon to serve their organization's customers and suppliers as well as organization members. Doing so offers potentially huge productivity and quality gains. One need only to look at the experience of organizations like General Electric, who increased its partnering initiatives with customers and suppliers while also making commitments to provide training and development opportunities as part of the partnering relationship. Training will also be needed for increasing numbers of people in telecommuting, part-time work, job sharing, apprenticeships, or other less than full-time permanent career work roles.

Blurred organizational boundaries and expanding worker roles will also result in the need for new training topics. For example, as organizations that have increasingly operated in a global environment have found out, their employees need training in other languages, cultures, and economic, political, and social issues affecting other nations. The increasing use of cross-functional teams will call for strategies to bridge cultural gaps between functions.

Perhaps even more radical than the expansion of content expectations for training will be the demand that products and services be delivered at the convenience of the customer. As long as classroom training is the dominant mode of delivery, customer convenience is an almost impossible goal to meet. The mechanics of delivering group training in a particular place at a particular time forces the participant to accommodate to the needs of the trainer. This is not much of a problem when organizations' training functions have essentially a captive audience. But as organizations have been willing to increasingly seek learning and development service on the open market, where price, quality, manner, and especially speed of delivery are the chief competitive factors, training functions are recognizing that the old way of doing their business will no longer work.

The classroom approach to training at the heart of most traditional training and development initiatives is ill-suited to this competitive arena. Customers of training want performance improvement; the traditional training model offers instruction with no guarantee of job transfer. Customers want individualized help; the traditional training orientation gives them one-size-fits-all. They want help on the job; they get it only in class. They want to control their own learning; trainers control the time, place, and content. They want highly specialized service; training simply cannot provide enough of it in a classroom mode where the economics work against small class sizes. They want contact with a wide range of experts and practical examples; the traditional training paradigm gives them a trainer or two and a small collection of case studies.

The reinvented approach to training must be aimed at delivering mass-customized, just-in-time learning and development services. This reinvented approach puts the focus on learning, not training, and this puts the learner at the center. The reinvented approach is flexible and adaptable in the sense that when learning is needed, it can be delivered anyplace at anytime. The reinvented approach allows customization to the individual and breaks down the boundary that classifies some training materials, situations, and settings as appropriate for learning while others are not.

To be successful, training professionals in today's and tomorrow's business environment requires individuals to plan, foresee, and premeditate not only the future of the business he or she is working for, but also the future of the profession. Organizations will continue to find themselves in the midst of tumultuous restructuring, reengineering, reinventing, and renewing processes in both the structure and leadership (and management) of their organizations. This should be of little surprise, since organizations during the past decade have been moving toward becoming flatter, less bureaucratic, less hierarchical, faster, and more responsive. In addition to these structural changes, organizations have also become more service-oriented, and are finding themselves relying more on the talent of their employees rather than the product they produce.

Kochan (1997) recently compiled, from a sampling of CEOs, the seven most significant business challenges caused by these changes:

1. Building and operating an effective customer responsive organization.
2. Gearing up for becoming an effective global competitor.
3. Competing profitably with low-cost providers.
4. Transitioning from a profit-through-cost-cutting to a revenue-growth environment.
5. Effectively taking advantage of new information technology.
6. Attracting, developing, and retaining top talent.
7. Operating internationally with the lack of competitive, probusiness industrial policy matching those of foreign competitors.

If these challenges are met effectively and successfully, an organization should see measurable improvements in areas such as increased coordination across functions, business units, and borders; employee commitment to continuous improvement; general management and leadership competence; creativity and entrepreneurship; and open communication (Beer 1997). However, to successfully meet and overcome these challenges requires changes in the area of HR and particularly in HRD and training.

Given the top seven challenges of CEOs, there is also a corresponding list of priorities or issues that training professionals should be addressing to ensure that these challenges are successfully navigated. These priorities overlap with our discussion thus far in this chapter:

1. Helping their organization reinvent or redesign itself to compete more effectively.
2. Reinventing the training function to be a more customer-focused, cost-justified function.
3. Training and developing the next generation—twenty-first century employees and leaders.
4. Contributing to the continuing cost containment–management effort.
5. Contributing to work on becoming a more effective business partner with their internal customers.
6. Rejecting fads, quick fixes, and other training fads and sticking to things that work.
7. Addressing the changing workforce challenge (i.e., diversity, part-time, and telecommuters).

CHANGING ORGANIZATIONAL STRUCTURES AND CAPABILITIES

The technology and KSAOCs needed by training professionals, organizational form and location, and mix of products and services must be continuously questioned by training professionals. Technology will continue to drive changes in the type of KSAOCs needed by training staff. Training professionals will need to get more and more comfortable with new technology and the notion that effective learning can happen without face-to-face classroom contact. This change in attitude is only the beginning. Instructional technology will continue to be a growing field, with subspecialties in such areas as graphics, animation, assembly of hypertext data bases, information networking, expert systems, and artificial intelligence. Every training professional will need to broaden and deepen their technology skills, and some will need highly specialized ones. The expectation that training staff will take on more roles of learning coach or consultant will continue as organizations find a greater need for people to help them become learning organizations.

Taking a more strategic, customer, performance improvement and accountability focus requires that the training function continue to reinvent its own operations. Dramatic reductions in cycle time (i.e., the time it takes from receipt of a request for training services until they can be delivered) will be aided by technology but will demand leaner, team-based training functions. There may well be fewer full-time training staff but a much wider network of part-time consultants, specialists, and contractors formed into project teams in the profession's own version of the virtual organization.

Technology, which until now has been used primarily to automate training management and to teach software skills, will become pervasive if we choose to make it so. Traditional classroom training will continue to move more toward integrating computers into instruction and use telecommunications and computers to bring learners into contact with a much wider array of experts and practical applications. This integration will come just-in-time as learners, especially younger people who have grown up in a multimedia environment, will demand higher quality and more entertainment in the computer-based learning services they receive. Learning services (expert advice, instruction, computer networks, and information databases) continue the movement toward being delivered to the same desktop computer that employees now use for word processing and electronic mail. The home, car, airport, and motel will also increasingly become learning sites when learning networks are linked to them via laptops, hand-held computers, and modems. Electronic performance support systems, in which learning is embedded in the performance of work tasks, will become more commonplace (Gery 1991).

Still further, training functions must continue to respond to the increased demand for a new focus on the question of how best to evaluate the effectiveness of training. How does one assess the contribution of training to achievement of an organization's strategic agenda, organizational problem solving, and organizational visioning, or to self-initiated, self-designed, and self-delivered learning and development services? It is clear that much more focus will continue to be needed on the learning and job or organizational impact types of evaluation, as opposed to reaction or "smile sheet" methods. Organizations must be willing to make a commitment to allocating the resources needed for more sophisticated evaluation and research designs. Training personnel will need to work to continue to develop expertise in these areas and find ways to gather formative data essential to providing better learning services. Senior leadership must demand more summative, ROI evaluation, and avoid the traditional tendency to support training largely on faith and anecdotal data. Such a demand will undoubtedly result in more sophisticated evaluations being actually used by training staff to evaluate training and development initiatives.

 Training functions will need to respond to increased calls for proving the value of training by focusing more on what training helps the organization accomplish and delivers given the organization's strategic agenda, and less on what training does. The training function will increasingly be judged on whether it enhances the organization's competitive advantage by adding real, noticeable economic value, not the perceived value of its activities. This is a difficult task for training personnel, because much of the training functions efforts have traditionally and continue to be hard to translate into economic terms—it is difficult to demonstrate to a manager why he or she should spend money on training when the benefits of the training are not clearly seen by the improvement of KSAOCs in the workforce or in a dollar amount of savings per year.

The training function of the future must place greater emphasis on benchmarking and showing leadership where the actual benefits of their training initiatives come from. Training functions can accomplish this by focusing more on organizational level outcomes and by developing tools to aid organizations in the new strategic directions they will be concentrating on in the future.

Training to Meet Internal HR–HRD Goals

A strategic and systematic approach to training in the future is necessary to ensure that the organization has knowledgeable, motivated, and efficient employees. These qualities will help to stabilize an organization's workforce, lower absenteeism, increase productivity, reduce operating costs, and develop employees to their fullest potential. Specific internal goals that training functions will need to continue to focus on in the future encompass a number of functional areas.

Recruitment and Orientation

Training will continue to have obvious links to internal recruitment, but it will also have an increased impact on promoting external recruitment. Training functions will be able to complement recruitment by helping identify the organization's future staffing and training needs given the strategic agenda; boost morale, which in turn reduces turnover; stabilize a workforce through retaining instead of hiring and firing employees; and reduce the amount of time needed for a new employee to become productive.

Career Planning and Employee Development

A proactive and responsible training function will continue to be a part of a career planning and employee development system, as training professionals keep a focus on ensuring the integration of training with career management. The training function will be able to accomplish this task by helping employees develop career paths and implement career planning consistent with the organizations and their own needs; preparing employees for special assignments, increasingly responsible jobs, and promotions; and guaranteeing the availability of qualified internal (and, where appropriate, external) replacements to fill jobs resulting from acquistions, diversification, and other organizational changes intended to improve competitive advantage.

Performance and Productivity

By facilitating performance and productivity goals, the training function will help contribute to cost control. The training function will be able to further performance and productivity in the organization in the following ways: assisting in redesigning jobs and developing job performance evaluation techniques that define relevant tasks and KSAOCs to learn for success in the job; increasing employee productivity while reducing overtime; decreasing breakage, waste, and maintenance costs; reducing the need for constant, close supervision as employees at all levels of the organization learn how to become leaders and effectively participate as members of self-directed work teams; improving communication among employees throughout the organization as boundaries and borders are eliminated; ensuring that skilled employees are available for expanding operations nationally and globally; and providing consultation on new policies for compensation and working conditions that assist the organization in better meeting its strategic agenda.

Training to Meet External HR Demands

Keeping pace with external forces that affect organizational goals will continue to be a challenge facing HR functions. A forward-looking training function will help its organization adapt to the ever-changing external environment. For example, like the trends discussed earlier in this chapter, the demands placed on organizations like "workforce 2000" will present unique training challenges for organizations.

Workforce 2000 suggests that the workforce will become older and will have a higher proportion of women and people of color. Training functions can give a competitive boost to their organizations by being prepared to address the training needs of minorities, women, and people with differing abilities who may never have had a real chance to compete in the labor market. Likewise, changes in the economy can change workforce composition and turnover rates; thus, training needs and training initiatives must be prepared to change accordingly. In addition, new laws and regulations will continue to create new training demands for organizations. The Americans With Disabilities Act and the Family and Medical Leave Act, and the Civil Rights Act of 1991, to name just a few examples, established mandates that often required new employee and management training programs to ensure compliance. There are no signs that new laws and regulations will not continue to place demands on training functions and their organizations.

Along with responding to external forces, training functions will need to become more adept at helping the organization and HR to anticipate needs before they arise. Awareness of technological advances and demographic changes in the labor market must guide the design of an organization's training function and responsibilities.

Anticipating Technological Change

As introduced earlier in this chapter, technology will continue to raise challenges for the training function and their organization. Every industry today is affected by the whirlwind pace of technology. Satellite communications, computers, word processors, and other technological aids will continue to help any employer become more competitive and productive. New financial theories, marketing strategies, and planning processes will also alter the way organizations do business. Organizations that do not adapt to these new processes and equipment are left behind, and as profits drop accordingly, they lose their competititive advantage.

As a result, the training function will continue to become more important than ever. To stay competitive, an organization will need to introduce new products or processes and services, or to relaunch existing products and services into new, and often global, marketplaces. The success of these initiatives in many instances will depend on the quality of training, learning, and development for line and staff in production, sales, and service.

Attracting a Quality Workforce

As demographic changes reshape the U.S. workforce, training functions must adapt to develop quality employees from the new marketplace. Some of the labor market projections that training personnel will need to keep in mind include the following.

Changing Profile of Entry-Level Workers. By the end of the decade, one out of three entry-level workers will be a member of a minority group.

Mismatch between Supply and Demand for Particular Job Categories. Certain job categories will experience uneven growth, and many companies will face chronic problems finding qualified workers for particular positions. Witness the difficulty many organizations are experiencing filling technology-oriented and knowledge worker jobs in recent years. As a result, training and retraining of workers will take on greater importance.

Increased Participation of Women in the Workplace. More and more women will continue to enter the workforce and pursue permanent careers. Already, growing numbers of women work full time, stay in their jobs for at least five years, and seek leadership positions. Nondiscrimination and elimination of the glass ceiling training for leaders, career development programs for women, and other forms of training must evolve to deal with this trend.

Growing Workforce Diversity. Organizations have recognized that diversity means not only more women and minorities in the workforce, but also new work values and ethics, and a more global workforce. For organizations to attract and retain qualified employees, training functions will need to take the lead in helping their organizations recognize and plan for this diversity.

Gaining and Maintaining Leadership Support for Training

Previously we have pointed out that many organizational leaders notice training costs but overlook the impact of training on organizational performance. To gain recognition for its strategic value, the training function will need to work at translating an organization's strategic goals into clear and achievable training objectives. To do so, the training function must become a strategic planning partner in top organization leadership.

As companies are increasingly recognizing the impact that training can have on organizational performance, training would do well to make sure they understand how their organization links training with strategic planning. That can be best accomplished by making sure that training leaders are included in the strategic planning process.

Training leaders should also understand what factors favor recognition of training's strategic value. Several criteria that demonstrate the inclusion of training in strategic planning are when adequate resources for training are allocated; training and other HR issues are given the same weight as other business issues; training is used for such things as quality management, team-building, and technical skill improvement; there is ongoing involvement of senior leaders in determining

mining training needs and involvement in subsequent training efforts; and training leaders have ongoing interaction with the organization's most senior leaders and HR leaders.

Sustaining a foothold in the echelons of top leadership will undoubtedly involve ongoing homework for training leaders. They must learn and understand the organization's strategic challenges so as to propose training and nontraining initiatives that can help address organizational problems, challenges, and opportunities. Training leaders (and other training staff) will continue to have a variety of ways for acquiring this business knowledge. They can acquire and read the organization's strategic plans, department plans, and other documents that describe the goals of each business unit. They can read books and industry journals in order to understand the organization's position in the marketplace. They can continue their own education and learning through internal and external courses to develop the KSAOCs necessary to understand and actively participate in the organization's business.

As training personnel increase their understanding and participation in the organization's and strategic challenges, they should actively be involved in developing plans that will highlight the ways in which the training function does and will promote and help achieve organizational objectives. By asking questions like the following, training personnel will be better able to make the link between organization strategy and training initiatives: What is the organization's basis business strategy and how does training fit in? How is training positioned within the organization and the marketplace? How can training help prepare employees to achieve the strategic agenda the organization wants? What are the most critical training initiatives that should be undertaken in the short- and long-term to support the strategic agenda? Who will oversee these initiatives and how will their value be measured? What are the training function's most critical assumptions about the organization's HRD needs?

Clearly, there will be an increasingly important role for the training profession in helping their organizations achieve objectives and sustain a competitive advantage. But those in the training profession must be willing to continue their recent efforts at reinventing the profession. And an important part of this reinvention must be continued efforts to link training to organizational strategy and build training's strategic value. The final section of this chapter presents a process for building training's strategic value to an organization.

BUILDING TRAINING'S STRATEGIC VALUE

The following process can help training staff enhance the training function's strategic value to the organization. The process is similar to the training audit (TA) discussed in Chapter 8, where organization and training personnel assess the overall training function and not just specific training initiatives.

Step 1: Specify Goals for the Training Function

Consider the organization's business conditions and be proactive in identifying specific training and nontraining practices to address these conditions. In developing goals statements, key questions to ask include the following:

- What are the organization's most critical sources of competitive advantage?
- What organization needs can the training function best meet through specific training practices?
- What payoff in time and money does the training function contribute to the organization? What would the organization gain or lose by eliminating or subcontracting training activities?
- What benefit do external customers receive from training initiatives?
- What benefit do internal customers receive from training initiatives?

Step 2: Assess the Performance of the Training Function and Its Staff

This step involves auditing current training practices and activities. In developing a strategic mission for the training function, key issues to address include the following:

- In which programs, activities, or efforts has training played a part? Did these activities have a positive or negative impact? What did training contribute to that outcome?
- Do training staff serve as specialists, generalists, partners, or pioneers?
- What are the training function's major strengths and weaknesses?

Step 3: State the Desired Capability of the Training Function

Consider the responses of Steps 1 and 2, and develop a vision for the training function by answering the following questions:

- What does training want its customers and employees to think and say about it?
- Why will training be important to the organization—now and in the future?
- How will training work to implement the vision?

Step 4: Prepare an Action Plan for Building Strategic Capability

Look at specific training activities and consider what actions training needs to take in each area to enhance the organization's overall strategic agenda:

1. *Staffing.* What competencies and KSAOCs does training need to bring into the function today? Tomorrow? What are the sources of these competencies and KSAOCs?
2. *Development.* What competencies and KSAOCs does training need to develop among its current staff? What actions must training take to ensure that its staff acquires these competencies and KSAOCs?
3. *Appraisal.* What standards does training need to develop? What feedback should it give to training professionals? How will training measure its success?
4. *Rewards.* What rewards can training use to motivate its staff to meet training goals?
5. *Function design.* What organization of training activities and reporting relationships will best allow the function to meet its strategic goals?
6. *Communication.* What information do individuals need to help the training function achieve its strategic mission?

Step 5: Prepare an Action for Building Training Professional Competencies and KSAOCs

This step highlights the personal competencies and KSAOCs needed by training professionals to serve in a strategic role. Four areas to address in personal action plans include the following:

1. *Activity.* What key activities can each person perform to contribute to the training function's capability?
2. *Time.* Where should the individual spend time to build the function's capability?
3. *Information.* What information does each staff member need to receive and/or share to build the function's capability?
4. *First steps.* What are the first steps each individual can take to effect a change?

Once the organization has agreed upon and established a strategic approach to training, they are positioned to ensure a better return on their investment in training.

CONCLUSION

The importance of training is likely to continue given recent trends in the workforce. Successful training in organizations depends on a reinvented training that involves a strategic approach, a careful needs analysis, and solid training program planning, design and evaluation. Reinvented training pays attention to designing learning environments that are attentive to characteristics of adult learners and principles of learning. Reinvented training recognizes the importance of using a variety of training methods in enhancing employee learning. Particular attention is given to changes in technology and its implications for learning and training delivery. When focusing on the training and development of leaders, a reinvented approach is attentive to the changing role of leaders, and the organizational expectations of those leaders.

Reinvented training recognizes the importance of an experiential learning approach to training and development design and the need to debrief the experiences of all training and development initiatives. Finally, reinvented training is committed to proving its value through benchmarking, ongoing evaluation, and energy focused on demonstrating the delivery of cost-effective training that meets customer objectives and contributes to the achievement of the organization's strategic agenda.

References and Bibliography

Allee, V. 1996. Adaptive organizations. *Executive Excellence, 3*: 20.

Allen, M. 1996. Training via computer on the rise. *National Underwriter Property and Casualty Risks and Benefits Management, 100* (42): 9, 28.

Alliger, G. M., & Janak, E. A. 1989. Kirkpatrick's levels of training criteria: Thirty years later. *Personnel Psychology, 42* (2): 331–342.

American Productivity & Quality Center. 1998. Leadership development: Building executive talent. *Consortium Benchmarking Study Proposal*. Alexandria, VA: ASTD.

American Psychological Association. 1979. Ethical standards of psychologists. *American Psychologist, 2*: 56–60.

American Society for Training and Development. 1997 industry report. *Training* (October): 44.

Argyris, C. 1982. *Reasoning, learning and action*. San Francisco: Jossey-Bass.

Aronson, R. B. 1996. Curtain call for CONDUIT. *Manufacturing Engineering, 117* (3): 70–72.

Bailey, D. A. 1990. Developing self-awareness through simulation and gaming. *Journal of Management Development, 9* (2): 38–42.

Baird, L., Briscoe, J., Tuden, L., & Rosansky, L. 1994. World class executive development. *Human Resource Planning, 16*: 1–16.

Bandura, A. 1977. *A social learning theory*. Englewood Cliffs, NJ: Prentice Hall.

Bardach, K. C. 1997. Patterns and trends in executive education. *Selections* (August): 18–25.

Barron, J. M., Berger, M. C., & Black, D. A. 1997. *On-the-job training*. Kalamazoo, MI: Upjohn Institute.

Becker, T. E., & Eveleth, D. M. 1995. Foci and bases of employee commitment: Implications for job performance. *Academy of Management Journal*, Best paper proceedings: 307–312.

Beer, M. 1997. The transformation of the HR function: Resolving tension between a traditional administrative and a new strategic role. *HRManagement, 36*: 49–56.

Bergmann, L. H., & Queen, T. R. 1987. The aftermath: Treating traumatic stress is crucial. *Corrections Today, 49* (5): 100–104.

Bernardin, H. J., & Russell, J. E. 1998. *Human resource management: An experiential approach.* Boston: Irwin McGraw-Hill.

Birnbauer, H. 1987. Evaluation techniques that work. *Training and Development Journal, 41* (1): 53–55.

Bolt, J. 1989. *Executive development: A strategy for corporate competitiveness.* New York: Harper & Row.

Borisoff, D., & Victor, D. 1989. *Conflict management: A communication skills approach.* Englewood Cliffs, NJ: Prentice Hall.

Bramley, P., & Hullah, H. 1987. Auditing training. *Journal of European Industrial Training, 11* (6): 5–10.

Brethower, S., & Rummler, G. A. 1979. Evaluating training. *Training and Development Journal, 33* (5): 14–22.

Breuer, N. L. 1992. AIDS issues haven't gone away. *Personnel Journal* (January): 47–49.

Brewington, E. L. 1996. *The ASTD training & development handbook.* 4th ed. New York: McGraw-Hill.

Broad, M. L., & Newstrom, J. W. 1992. *Transfer of training: Action-packed strategies to ensure high payoff from training investments.* Reading, MA: Addison-Wesley.

Buckley, R., & Caple, J. 1984. The training audit. *Journal of European Industrial Training, 8* (7): 3–8.

Burack, E. H., Hochwarter, W., & Mathys, N. J. 1997. The new management development paradigm. *Human Resource Planning, 20* (1): 14–28.

Butler, F. C. 1978. The concept of competence: An operational definition. *Educational Technology, 18* (1): 7–18.

Byrne, D. 1969. Attitudes and attraction. In L. Berkowitz (Ed.), *Advances in experimental social psychology* (pp. 35–90). New York: Academic Press.

Cannell, M. 1997. Practice makes perfect. *People Management, 3* (5): 26–33.

Cappelli, P., & Crocker-Hefter, A. 1996. Distinctive human resources are firms' core competencies. *Organizational Dynamics, 3*: 7–22.

Chatham, J. 1989. Improving interactional organizational research: A model of person/organization fit. *Academy of Management Review, 14*: 333–349.

Cleveland, H. 1985. *The knowledge executive.* New York: E. P. Dutton.

Crichton, M. 1992. *Rising sun.* New York: Knopf.

De Nicola, N. 1990. Debriefing sessions: The missing link in focus groups. *Marketing News, 24* (1): 20–22.

DeWine, S. 1994. *The consultant's craft: Improving organizational communication.* New York: St. Martin's Press.

Digman, L. 1980. Determining management development needs. *Human resource management* (Winter): 12–17.

Dionne, P. 1996. The evaluation of training activities: A complex issue involving different stakes. *Human Resource Development Quarterly, 7* (3): 279–286.

Dowling, P., & Welch, F. 1991. The strategic adaptation process in international human resources management: A case study. *Human Resource Planning, 1*: 61–69.

Emory, C. W., & Cooper, D. R. 1991. *Business research methods.* 4th ed. Burr Ridge, IL: Irwin.

Estabrooke, R. M., & Fay, N. F. 1992. Answering the call of "tailored training." *Training* (October): 29, 85–88.

Faerman, S. R., & Ban, C. 1993. Trainee satisfaction and training impact: Issues in training evaluation. *Public Productivity & Management Review, 16* (3): 299–314.

Filipczak, B. 1996. Who owns your OJT? *Training, 33* (12): 44–49.

Ford, J. 1993. Benchmarking HRD. *Training and Development Journal* (June): 36–41.

Francis, D., & Woodcock, M. 1990. *Unblocking organizational values.* Glenview, IL: Scott Foresman.

Furnham, A. 1997. Fire the training department. *Across the Board* (March): 9–10.

Galpin, T. J. 1996. *The human side of change.* San Francisco: Jossey-Bass.

Garvin, D. A. 1993. Building a learning organization. *Harvard Business Review* (July–August): 78–92.

Gaw, B. A. 1979. Processing questions: An aid to completing the learning cycle. In J. E. Jones & J. W. Pfeiffer (Eds.), *The 1979 annual handbook for group facilitator* (pp. 147–153). La Jolla, CA: University Associates.

Gentry, J. W. 1990. What is experiential learning? In J. Gentry (Ed.), *Guide to business gaming and experiential learning* (pp. 9–20). London: Nichols/GP.

Gery, G. 1996. *Electronic performance support systems.* Boston: Weingarten Publications.

———. 1991. *Electronic performance support systems: How and why to remake the workplace through the strategic application of technology.* Boston: Weingarten Publications.

Gitter, R. J. 1994. Apprenticeship-trained workers: United States and Great Britain. *Monthly Labor Review* (April): 38–43.

Goldstein, I. L. 1986. *Training in organizations: Needs assessment, development, and evaluation.* 2nd ed. Monterey, CA: Brooks-Cole.

Gomez-Mejia, L. R., Balkin, D. B., & Cardy, R. L. 1998. *Managing human resources.* Englewood Cliffs, NJ: Prentice Hall.

Gordon, J., & Hequet, M. 1997. Live and in person. *Training* (November): 24–31.

Greco, J. 1997. Long-distance learning. *Journal of Business Strategy, 18* (3): 53–54.

Grove, D. A., & Ostroff, C. 1990. Training program evaluation. In K. N. Wexley & J. R. Hinrichs (Eds.), *Developing human resources.* Washington, D.C.: Bureau of National Affairs.

Gunz, H. P. 1995. Realism and learning in management simulations. *Journal of Management Education, 19* (1): 54–74.

Gupta, A. 1992. Executive searches: A strategic perspective. *Human Resource Planning, 1*: 47–61.

Gutteridge, T., Leibowitz, Z., & Shore, J. 1993. A new look at organizational career development. *Human Resource Planning, 16*: 71–83.

Hamblin, A. C. 1970. Evaluation of training. *Industrial Training International* (November): 25–37.

Hawthorne, E. M. 1987. *Evaluating training programs*. Westport, CT: Greenwood.

Henry, J. 1989. Measuring and practice in experiential learning. In S. Well & I. McGill (Eds.), *Making sense of experiential learning: Diversity in theory and practice* (pp. 25–37). Bristol, PA: Open University Press.

Hilgard, E. R., & Bower, G. A. 1996. *Theories of learning*. New York: Appleton-Century-Crofts.

Hoover, J. D., & Whitehead, C. J. 1975. An experiential–cognitive methodology in the first course in management: Some preliminary results. In R. H. Buskirk (Ed.), *Simulation games and experiential learning in action* (pp. 25–30).

Howard, R. 1992. The CEO as organizational architect: An interview with Xerox's Paul Allaire. *Harvard Business Review* (September–October): 22–30.

Howes, P., & Foley, P. 1993. Strategic human resource management: An Australian case study. *Human Resource Planning, 3*: 53–64.

Informationweek. 1997. Computer-based training enters the mainstream—CBT Group shows strong growth as it makes impact with big companies, 27 January, 140.

Ivancevich, J. M. 1998. *Human resource management*. Boston: Irwin McGraw-Hill.

Johnson, W. B., & Packer, A. H. 1987. *Workforce 2000*. Indianapolis: The Hudson Institute.

Judge, T., & Ferris, G. 1992. The elusive criterion of fit in human resource staffing decision. *Human Resource Planning, 15*: 47–67.

Kaplan, R. S., & Norton, D. P. 1992. The balanced scorecard—Measures that drive performance. *Harvard Business Review* (January–February): 71–79.

Katz, D., & Kahn, R. L. 1978. *The social psychology of organizations*. New York: John Wiley & Sons.

Kirkpatrick, D. L. 1996. Great ideas revisited. *Training and Development* (January): 54–59.

———. 1994. *Evaluating training programs: The four levels*. San Francisco: BerrettKoehler.

Klepper, W. 1994. Adapted from Columbia University Graduate School of Business Course, *Managing Groups and Interpersonal Dynamics.*

Kochan, T. 1997. Rebalancing the role of HR. *HRManagement, 36*: 121–127.

Kolb, D. A. 1984. *Experiential learning: Experience as the source of learning and development*. Englewood Cliffs, NJ: Prentice Hall.

Kolb, D. A., & Lewis, L. H. 1986. Facilitating experiential learning: Observations and reflections. In L. H. Lewis (Ed.), *Experiential and simulation techniques for teaching adults* (pp. 99–107). San Francisco: Jossey-Bass.

Kolb, D. A., Osland, J. S., & Rubin, I. M. 1995. *Organizational behavior: An experiential approach*. 6th ed. Englewood Cliffs, NJ: Prentice Hall.

Kotter, J. 1996. *Leading change*. Boston: Harvard Business School Publishing.

Kruse, K. 1997. Five levels of Internet-based training. *Training and Development* (February): 60–61.

Laschinger, H. K., & Boss, M. W. 1984. Learning styles in nursing students and career choices. *Journal of Advanced Nursing, 9*: 375–380.

Lederman, L. C. 1992. Debriefing: Toward a systematic assessment of theory and practice. *Simulation & Gaming, 23* (2): 145–159.

Lederman, L. C., & Stewart, L. P. 1986. *Instructional manual for THE MARBLE COMPANY: A simulation board game.* New Brunswick, NJ: SCILS.

Lee, R. 1996. The "pay-forward" view of training. *People Management, 2* (3): 30–32.

Mager, R. F., & Pipe, P. 1984. *Analyzing performance problems: Or, you really oughta wanna.* Belmont, CA: David Lake Publishing.

Manis, M. 1966. *Cognitive processes.* Monterey, CA: Brooks/Cole.

Marsick, V., Cederholm, L., Turner, E., & Pearson, T. 1992. Action–reflection learning. *Training and Development* (August): 63–66.

Mastaglio, T. W., & Callahan, R. 1995. A large scale complex virtual environment for team training. *Computer, 28*: 49–56.

Mathieu, J. E., & Leonard, R. L. 1987. Applying utility concepts to a training program in supervisory skills: A time-based approach. *Academy of Management Journal, 30*: 316–335.

Mathis, R. L., & Jackson, J. H. 1991. *Personnel/Human resource mangement.* St. Paul: West.

McCall, M., Lombardo, M., & Morrison, A. 1988. *The lessons of experience.* Lexington, MA: Lexington Books.

McCart, C. L., Toombs, W., Lindsay, C., & Crowe, M. B. 1985. *Learning styles among established professionals.* Paper presented at 1985 AERA Conference, Chicago.

McGehee, W., & Thayer, P. W. 1961. *Training in business and industry.* New York: John Wiley.

McKenna, J. F. 1992. Apprenticeships: Something old, something new, something needed. *Industry Week* (20 January): 14–20.

Middleton, T. 1992. The potential of virtual reality technology for training. *Journal of Interactive Instructional Development* (Spring): 8–11.

Mills, J. 1976. A procedure for explaining experiments involving deception. *Personality and Social Psychology Bulletin, 2*: 3–13.

Minehan, M. 1996. Virtual reality: The next step in training. *HR Magazine* (August): 144–153.

Mirabile, R. J. 1991. Pinpointing development needs: A simple approach to skills assessment. *Training & Development, 45*: 19–25.

Mishan, E. J. 1976. *Cost–benefit analysis.* New York: Praeger.

Mondy, R. W., & Noe, R. M. 1990. *Human resource management.* 4th ed. Boston: Allyn & Bacon.

Monoky, J. F. 1996. Master the coaching call. *Industrial Distribution, 85* (6): 112.

Moses, J. L., & Byham, W. C., eds. 1977. *Applying the assessment center method.* New York: Pergamon.

Mullaney, C. A., & Trask, L. D. 1992. Show them the ropes. *Technical and Skills Training* (October): 8–11.

Mullen, T., & Lyles, M. 1993. Toward improving management's contribution to organizational learning. *Human Resource Planning, 16*: 35–49.

Murphy, J. R. 1997. Results first, change second. *Training, 34* (5): 58–64.

Nai, A. K. 1994. The latest addition to the executive suite is the psychologist's couch. *Wall Street Journal*, 29 August, 1.

Nissen, A. B., & Ransom, L. S. 1983. Group debriefings: Peer assistance for the physically challenged student. *Journal of Cooperative Education, 20* (1): 106–112.

Nunally, J. 1978. *Psychometric theory*. 2nd ed. New York: McGraw-Hill.

Osbaldeston, M., & Barham, K. 1992. Using management development for competitive advantage. *Long Range Planning, 6*: 18–24.

Overman, S. 1995. Japan shares ways to improve job training. *HR Magazine* (January): 60, 62, 64.

Packham, R., Roberts, R., & Bawden, R. 1989. Our faculty goes experiential. In S. Weil & I. McGill (Eds.), *Making sense of experiential learning* (pp. 129–149). Bristol, PA: Open University Press.

Pearson, M., & Smith, D. 1986. Debriefing in experience-based learning. *Simulation/Games for Learning, 16* (4): 155–172.

Peterson, G. W., & Stakenas, R. G. 1981. Performance-based education: Method for preserving quality, equal opportunity, and economy in public higher education. *Journal of Higher Education, 52* (4): 352–368.

Petranek, C., Corey, S., & Black, R. 1992. Three levels of learning in simulations: Participating, debriefing, and journal writing. *Simulation and Gaming, 23* (2): 174–185.

Phillips, J. J. 1997. A rational approach to evaluating training programs . . . including calculating ROI. *The Journal of Lending & Credit Risk Management, 79* (11): 43–50.

———. 1996. *Accountability in Human Resource Management*. Houston: Gulf Publishing Company.

Phipps, P. A. 1996. On-the-job training and employee productivity. *Monthly Labor Review, 119* (3): 3.

Pierre, D. 1996. The evaluation of training activities: A complex issue involving different stakes. *Human Resource Development Quarterly, 7* (3): 279.

Plant, R. A., & Ryan, R. J. 1992. Training evaluation: A procedure for validating an organization's investment in training. *Journal of European Industrial Training, 16* (10): 22–38.

Prahalad, C., & Hamel, G. 1990. The core competence of the corporation. *Harvard Business Review* (May–June): 277–299.

Psotka, J. 1995. Immersive training systems: Virtual reality and education and training. *Instructional Science, 23*: 405–431.

Reynolds, L. 1993. Apprenticeship program raises many questions. *HR Focus* (July): 1, 4.

Robinson, D. G., & Robinson, J. 1995. *Performance consulting: Moving beyond training*. San Francisco, CA: Berrett-Koehler.

Robinson, G., & Wick, C. 1992. Executive development that makes a business difference. *Human Resource Planning, 15*: 63–75.

Rothwell, W. J. 1996. *Beyond training and development: State-of-the-art strategies for enhancing human performance*. New York: AMACOM.

Rothwell, W. J., & Kazanas, H. C. 1993. *The complete AMA guide to management development*. New York: AMACOM.

Schein, E. 1990. Organizational culture. *American Psychologist, 45*: 109–119.

Senge, P. M. 1990a. The leaders' new work: Building learning organizations. *Sloan Management Review* (Fall): 7–23.

Senge, P. M. 1990b. *The fifth discipline.* New York: Doubleday.

Shandler, D. 1996. *Reengineering the training function.* Delray Beach, FL: St. Lucien Press.

Shaw, D., & Schneider, C. 1993. Making organizational change happen: The keys to successful delayering. *Human Resource Planning, 16*: 1–17.

Sims, R. R. 1993. *Training enhancement in government organizations.* Westport, CT: Quorum Books.

Sims, R. R., Veres, J. G., & Shake, L. 1989. An exploratory examination of the convergence between the learning style questionnaire and the revised learning style inventory. *Educational and Psychological Measurement, 49* (3): 227–233.

Smith, C. 1993. The executive's new coach. *Fortune, 27* (December): 126–134.

Smith, D. M., & Kolb, D. A. 1986. *User's guide for the learning style inventory.* Boston: McBer.

Sonntag, E. 1997. Emerging PC training technologies. Http://www.trainingnet.com

Stamps, D. 1997. Mercedes-Benz sows a learning field. *Training* (March): 26–32.

Stufflebeam, D., Foley, W., Gepart, W., Guba, E., Hammong, R., Merriman, H., & Provus, M. 1971. *Educational evaluation and decision making.* Itasca, IL: Peacock.

Suchman, E. 1967. *Evaluating research.* New York: Russell Sage.

Swierczek, F. W., & Carmichael, L. 1985. The quantity and quality of evaluating training. *Training and Development Journal, 14* (3): 95–99.

Tannenbaum, S. I., & Woods, S. B. 1992. Determining a strategy for evaluating training: Operating within organizational constraints. *Human Resource Planning, 15* (2): 63–81.

Tennen, H., & Gillen, R. 1979. The effect of debriefing on laboratory induced helplessness: An attributional analysis. *Journal of Personality, 47*: 629–642.

Thatcher, D. 1986. Promoting learning through games and simulations. *Simulation/Games for Learning, 16* (4): 144–154.

Thatcher, D., & Robinson, M. J. 1990. Me—the slow learner: Reflections eight years on from its original design. *Simulation & Gaming, 21*: 291–302.

Thiagarajan, S. 1992. Using games for debriefing. *Simulation & Gaming, 23* (2): 161–173.

Training. 1997. Correction to last year's industry report (October): 39–46.

Ulrich, D. 1992. Strategic human resource planning: Linking customers and employees. *Human Resource Planning, 15*: 47–81.

Ulrich, D., & Lake, D. 1990. *Organizational capability: Competing from the inside/out.* New York: John Wiley & Sons.

Veres, J. G., Sims, R. R., & Locklear, T. 1991. Improving the reliability of Kolb's revised learning style inventory. *Educational and Psychological Measurement, 51* (1): 143–150.

Verlander, E. G. 1992. Executive education for managing complex organizational learning. *Human Resource Planning, 15* (2): 1–18.

Vicere, A. A. 1992. The strategic leadership imperative for executive education. *Human Resource Planning, 15* (1): 16–31.

Vicere, A. A., & Fulmer, R. M. 1998. *Leadership by design.* Boston: Harvard Business School Press.

————. 1996. *Crafting competitiveness: Developing leaders in the shadow pyramid.* Oxford, UK: Capstone Publishing.

Wagenheim, G., & Gemmill, G. 1994. Feedback exchange: Managing group closure. *Journal of Management Education, 18* (2): 265–269.

Walker, G. 1990. Crisis-care in critical incident debriefing. *Death Studies, 14*: 121–133.

Walters, G. A., & Marks, S. E. 1981. *Experiential learning and change: Theory and practice.* New York: John Wiley & Sons.

Walters, G. M. 1997. Molding tomorrow's managers. *Across the Board, 34* (8): 55.

Warrick, D. D., Hunsacker, P., Cook, C. W., & Altman, S. 1979. Debriefing experiential learning exercises. *Journal of Experiential Learning and Simulation, 1* (2): 98–100.

Wexley, K. N., & Latham, G. P. 1991. *Developing and training human resources in organizations.* New York: HarperCollins.

Wick, C., & Leon, L. 1993. *The learning edge.* New York: McGraw-Hill.

Wiley, J. 1997. CBT evolves. *Air Transport World, 34* (4): 81–83.

Willyerd, K. A. 1997. Balancing your evaluation act. *Training, 34* (3): 52–57.

Wolfe, D. 1980. Developing professional competence in the applied behavioral sciences. *New Directions for Experiential Learning, 8*: 1–16.

Zuboff, S. 1988. *In the age of the smart machine: The future of work and power.* New York: Basic Books.

Index

ABOUT THE AUTHOR

RONALD R. SIMS is the Floyd Dewey Gottwald Senior Professor of Business Administration, College of William & Mary, where he teaches organizational behavior, human resource management, leadership, and management of change. Author of more than 70 articles in the journals of his field, his most recent Quorum books include *Human Resource Management and the Americans with Disabilities Act* (with John G. Veres, III) (1995), *Changes and Challenges for the Human Resource Professional* (with Serbrenia J. Sims) (1994), and *Ethics and Organizational Decision Making: A Call for Renewal* (1994).